WESTERN
BOXING
AND
WORLD
WRESTLING

WESTERN BOXING AND WORLD WRESTLING

STORY AND PRACTICE

BY
JOHN F. GILBEY

 NORTH ATLANTIC BOOKS, BERKELEY, CALIFORNIA

Western Boxing and World Wrestling: Story and Practice

Copyright © 1986, 1993 by John F. Gilbey. No portion of this book, except for brief review, may be reproduced in any form without written permission of the publisher. For information contact North Atlantic Books.

Published by
North Atlantic Books
P.O. Box 12327
Berkeley, California 94701

Cover and book design by Paula Morrison
Typeset by Catherine Campaigne
Printed in the United States of America

Western Boxing and World Wrestling: Story and Practice is sponsored by the Society for the Study of Native Arts and Sciences, a nonprofit educational corporation whose goals are to develop an educational and cross-cultural perspective linking various scientific, social, and artistic fields; to nurture a holistic view of arts, sciences, humanities, and healing; and to publish and distribute literature on the relationship of mind, body, and nature.

Library of Congress Cataloging-in-Publication Data
Gilbey, John F.
    Western boxing and world wrestling
    Includes bibliographical references
    1. Boxing—History. 2. Wrestling—History.
3. Boxers (Sports)—Biography. 4. Wrestlers—Biography
I. Title.
GV1121.S65   1986   796.8'3   86-5254
ISBN 0-938190-73-3
ISBN 0-938190-72-5 (pbk.)

Table of Contents

Foreword

After the publication of my first two books, *Secret Fighting Arts of the World*, (1963) and *The Way of a Warrior* (1982), several correspondents wrote asking about my experiences in Western boxing and wrestling. I had already written some chapters bearing on these sports through the years and so with some effort and no little interruption from my business schedule I pushed this work through to completion. The literature on both boxing and wrestling, though extensive, is uneven and inaccurate and the job took some muscle. My own tome doesn't pretend to be a definitive analysis. I'll leave that to stoop-shouldered historians whose lives are in the library stacks. Mine, happily, is in the streets. All I want to do here is to trace these sports' beginnings and development and, particularly, to discuss their rationale and the fighters who peopled them. As always, my hope is that readers will move on to enjoy and learn. Finally, I want to thank Con Warren and Jonathan Laing for help with the text, and Pat Kennedy for the graphics that adorn the text.

WESTERN PUGILISM AND BOXING

I've watched the seconds pat and nurse
Their man; and seen him put to bed;
With twenty guineas in his purse,
And not an eye within his head.
                                        —J. H. Reynolds

The Best Western Boxer

The best western boxer I ever saw you never heard of. Unless you were intimate with amateur boxing lore around Peoria in the 1930's. Right. Andy Jones was an amateur, but don't hold that against him—some of the greatest fighters for one reason or another never fought pro. The Britisher Harold W. Mallin, for in-

---

Representative books used in preparing this chapter were: J. Babcock, *The Fancy*, 1826; A. Bass et al, *Medical Aspects of Boxing*, 1965; Bob Burrill, *Who's Who in Boxing*, 1973; H. E. Cleveland, *Fisticuffs and Personalities of the Ring*, ca. 1920; Pierce Egan, *Boxiana*, 1818–48; Nat Fleischer, *Black Dynamite*, 1947; Nat Fleischer, *50 Years at Ringside*, 1958; W. C. Heinz, *The Fireside Book of Boxing*, 1961; E. Jokl, *The Medical Aspect of Boxing*, 1941; A. Liebling, *The Sweet Science*, 1956; J. C. Reid, *Bucks and Bruisers*, 1971; *The 1985 Ring Encyclopedia and Record Book*; A. Roberts, *Brain Damage in Boxers*, 1969; F. G. Shaw, *The Science of Self Defense*, 1919; T. B. Shepherd, *The Noble Art*, 1950; and E. Summerskill, *The Ignoble Art*, 1956.

stance, went undefeated in more than three hundred bouts early this century.

I cry a lot these days. (There's nothing wrong with it. We should cry more. To hell with Kid Macho. Aeneas, Hector, Beowulf, Roland, and Lancelot blubbered like school-girls, so why shouldn't we? And Chesterton, who was smarter than all of us, believed that it was a weak nation whose warriors couldn't cry.) Every time Holmes dances for another million I think of good boxers who starved. And when I see the exploiters and "champions" in the karate/kung fu charade, my handkerchief works overtime. When American and European so-called fighters with marcelled hairdoes and their armpits de-sweat glanded, strut around accompanied by chauffeurs and bodyguards and basketfuls of money, you have to ask what the hell this has to do with fighting. Glamor and fighting seldom marry. Fighting is a tough trade and is as distant from Hollywood sets as Tierra del Fuego.

What really hurts is that some very skilled men not too long ago couldn't make a dime with their tremendous tools, while these frauds shamelessly exploit their sorry skills. I don't blame them. I blame the public. After all, half the people in this republic actually think Sylvester Stallone is a boxer. They probably think he's a patriot too, whereas he spent the war as a chaperone at a girls' school in Switzerland.

Andy Jones was a featherweight amateur boxer (126 lbs.) who fought light-heavies. I've even seen him train with full-fledged heavies and run 'em through the ropes.

I never saw him lose. And I never even saw him sit down between rounds. He was so good he wasn't above show-boating with a middleweight. He had TNT in each fist and a variety of punches the like of which I've seen no boxer—amateur or pro— possess. He had all the moves, and could box from a right as effectively as from a left stance.

Andy fought good and he fought clean. He wasn't above carrying an opponent if the whim hit him and he wanted some exercise. (A good fighter can carry a bad one, get round-shouldered doing it, and the crowd never knows. Sugar Ray Robinson once fought Charlie Fusari for charity. Afterwards Ray commented:

"It was my toughest fight. I had to fight 15 rounds for me and 15 for him.") But let a guy try to use his thumbs or rabbit-punch him, Andy would take him out quickly—but cleanly. He wasn't like Mae West ("When I'm good, I'm good, but when I'm bad I'm better"), he was so good he didn't have to fight dirty. And his sense of ethics was such that even if he had been less efficient he still would not have gone the Fritzie Zivic-Bummy Davis route.

Andy was humane. If he cut a man's eye, he would never exploit it. Instead he'd dig for the body.

"Ain't no art in tearing a cut open further," he said, "anyone can do it. He's gonna have enough trouble with the eye without your fist in it. Real test for you then is to go elsewhere, work on something else."

As I said, Andy was the best I ever saw for his age, poundage, and quality of competition. If he had turned pro I am convinced he would have been another Joe Gans.

So what happened? Why didn't he become champion of the world? Was he so punchy from the overweight matches that it finally got to him? No, it wasn't that. True, he took punishment by fighting the big boys, but he had to—he was so superior in his own weight he couldn't get a fight. But he wasn't punchy.

No, the trouble was a woman—his wife, Sally. He promised her each year he'd quit but he kept going, often fighting for a cheap watch or $2 a round for three-rounders. And when the big city managers started coming around with offers she continued to worry for her warhorse, afraid if he left the foundry he'd bomb out with the big town pros and come home broke and broken.

You say this was a no-faith gal? You couldn't be wronger. Sally was a woman all of us should have. Happy and singing always. But heck, jobs were hard to get then, and blacks got them last. She knew he was a good man and she guessed he was a great boxer but with her woman's instinct she sensed the jungle outside and it scared her.

Sally worried a lot but she was no termagant. She had four qualities absent in a fishwife: quietness, humor, endurance, and of course love. The love she had for Andy was the sort you get in Galsworthy's "The Apple Tree" and Zweig's "Letter From an

Unknown Woman." Or the kind that great vocalists like Bessie Smith, Billie Holiday, and Helen Morgan sang about. Fact is, Sally was the kind of woman who believed the words of those songs. And these, brothers and sisters, were women of depth.

She didn't have to work at being a woman—she was one. She could get more exercise just walking across a room than most gals get in a couple of sets of tennis. She was aware of her body and it was good to her, but she never used it coquettishly. It was just her and a part of being vibrantly alive . . .

And in love. They basked in it. Their smiles always had a future in them. It was good just to be around them. I was just a youngster, not dry behind the ears yet, training with Andy but I could see and sense this magnificent thing.

But boxing marred it; maybe not a lot but it created a tension where before there had been only resonance. It wasn't that she was jealous of it. When he began pushing the gloves, in fact, she welcomed it as a needed recreation for a guy who came home sagging from the hard labor of a foundry. She willingly shared him with this new interest; it let him tap-dance the "tired" out, let him shag, she'd say, instead of sag.

Sally didn't really get bothered by boxing until Andy had cleaned up all the eligible featherweights in a three-state area and was taking on the big 'uns. By then he had a reputation and at little cost—most fights he didn't get his hair mussed.

But as time went on he took some punishment. He was too fast for a middleweight but his arms took a beating and he'd come home weary from being manhandled in the clinches by the superior weight. This Sally didn't like and as nicely as she could she asked him to give it up.

He didn't refuse—he loved her too much for that—but he delayed her and she let him. After all, the undefeated record had not changed him. He was the same simple laughing lovable guy she'd married, a beautiful bozo. If he'd become proud she would have stopped the boxing instanter, but he stayed her sweet little man. But eventually her quiet (as he left for and returned from a fight) came to hurt him more than the punches the big boys were throwing. And so he chucked it. After that he settled for

6   *John F. Gilbey*

training some of the youngsters around town.

After he quit, I got a short letter from him that I still cherish.

> Sally's a good woman. So nice. She loves music and nature and
> life. And me—don't ask me why. Me a foundry flunky. But that
> never mattered to her. Every day she dances for me.
>
> The one thing I was good at—boxing—she didn't like. So
> I've finally given it up. But don't feel sorry for me John. Some
> may say a pug like me is too stupid to be unhappy. No, I'm too
> smart. How many folks have a good and loving wife? I got rid
> of boxing and I kept her. I never had a college education but
> you don't need one to know when you're loved. I got me a girl!

Dick Corbett was a home town boy in Andy's weight class
who didn't last out the opening round the first time they met.
Dick moved to Chicago after that and in a few years had cut
himself quite a swath in the available supply of amateur featherweights and lightweights. Dick was a boxer-cum-slugger. Decep-
tive, he shuffled flat-footed like Joe Louis but he was dandy slipping punches and riding crosses.

Inevitably, these two met again, at a big show in Peoria. Dick
was superb that night but withal putty in Andy's hands and lost
a one-sided decision after barely finishing.

In the regional Golden Gloves tournament that year Dick
purposely added pounds, moved up to the lightweights, and took
the championship, winning every bout by knockout. He needn't
have dodged by moving up to a heavier weight: Andy came down
with flu and didn't even fight.

Before long Dick turned pro and packed off to New York City.
He moved up the rankings in two or three years, winning every
bout, most of them by knockout.

The summer Dick got ranked fifth best lightweight in the
world he returned in triumph to Peoria. I was in Chicago at the
time and I got a call from Andy: could I come down?

I went to Peoria and met him in a dive on Jefferson Street.
A rendezvous there seemed strange but as soon as I sat down in
a back booth and he began to talk I saw why we were meeting
away from his home.

"Corbett's back," he starts.

"Oh," from me.

"He's got quite a record."

I took some beer slowly, looking at him, wondering where this was going. I put the glass down. "Yeah, I've been following him. He's doing okay."

"He wants to fight me."

He said it uncertainly, almost like a little boy telling his dad that he'd blown the rent money on a sled. It was so uncharacteristic of him, that I had trouble getting my head and tongue to work.

"How can that be?" I finally blurted out; "You retired as an amateur three years ago."

Then he told it all to me. Corbett's return home was ostensibly to glory in the adulation of the local fans, but what he'd really come for was to remove the only two blots on his record, those losses in past years to Andy. He told Andy on the phone that he was not angry, that it was strictly a matter of principle—he wanted to clean up his record. Andy, with Sally preparing a meal in the kitchen, thought fast, got his number, and said he'd ring him back. That's where we were.

"What do I do?" he asked.

"Hell," I came on powerful now, "you don't do anything. You retired as an amateur feather three years ago. You're in lousy shape. Corbett's a professional lightweight and trained to precision. It's a silly proposition. Give me his phone number and I'll lay it out solid and simple so he'll understand." I was peeved.

"I can beat him, John," he said with a smile.

"You probably could," I rejoined, "but what's the percentage, what do you get out of it except pain?"

"He's offered me a cool thousand just to fight, double that if I win. That's far more money than I made in eighty fights."

I eyed him, "Do you need the money? I can round up a thousand for you in three days. A gift from a buddy."

"Nope, I don't need it. No, it's not the money. I want to do it, but I don't know how to describe why. I guess it's for boxing. The thrill of those gloves, the sweat, the getting and the giving. And yes, even the pain. Boxing and Sally have been my life. Do you understand?"

I understood and told him so. "But what about Sally?"

His eyes lowered to the table top and he fiddled with his glass. "I told her I quit, but I never told her I would never fight again. She won't like it. I won't attempt to hide it afterward, only before. That's why I need you. Will you make the arrangements and referee the thing?"

"Sally's going to hate me," I hesitated.

"I'll handle that part of it. You make the match. The sooner the better."

Sooner was the next day at 5 p.m. in an old buff's garage on the outskirts of town. This bird had been training Golden Glovers for years and he knew Andy well and could keep quiet. I made him take a c-note.

Corbett looked grand in street clothes. I knew I'd have some misgivings when he got into his boxing trunks, but hell, I wasn't fighting him.

It turned out I was right—he looked like hell, which is to say damned good. Andy had greeted him quietly. Corbett was polite, but his vibes were like steel darts.

We got their hand wraps and eight-ounce gloves on and then I said to Corbett: "The regular three three-minute rounds, a minute's breather in between?"

"Nope," he says coldly, "we go till there's a winner."

I started to expostulate and Andy waved me off. "It's okay John; let's get started."

This simplified the refereeing chore. Since both were clean fighters I wasn't sure what role I was to play in the ruckus. So I ad-libbed, got them to touch gloves, and moved back.

And a ruckus it was. Corbett came out stiff jabbing with his left and crossing with his right. The first few he threw weren't meaningful. But then he got crisp as a fresh cracker. Andy moved easily, rolling well with the punches and, when Corbett overpressed, caught him with a beautiful uppercut. It was timed so well that it would have toppled the old Corbett, but the new one just blinked his eyes and continued to whipsaw.

Andy kept him off but didn't throw much. And you couldn't

safely leave Corbett in front of you throwing leather from every angle without blunting him. Still, Andy lay back, slipping and ducking without a counter. Corbett, chalking it up to the rust of non-training, was emboldened and stepped up the attack. And he started to connect. One shot, two, three. Still no riposte.

Ten minutes had gone by and Andy still weathered the storm, but he seemed to be tiring. Then Corbett got in a rocking left jab, buckling Andy's knees. Corbett followed in with a right cross that Andy only partially blocked and then, pivoting, Corbett shot a left hook toward Andy's jaw. A classic sequence, the kind Georges Carpentier was famed for.

But Carpentier got beat by the Dixie Kid remember? And the Kid was the best going at pretending to be out on his feet, luring you close, and finishing you.

Andy did a Dixie Kid. He absorbed Corbett's left jab, letting his legs sag, got only a little of his glove on the incoming right cross, and then when Corbett brought around the left hook, Andy stepped inside it with a potent right that couldn't have traveled six inches.

Corbett fell right on my right foot and didn't stir for a full minute. I gave him some smelling salts and he came up groggy.

"We continue," he rasped, staggering around.

Then *I* took over. "If you do, Andy will kill you. And I won't let him. If you force it you get to him only through me and I'm two hundred pounds and dying to tear you apart."

That stopped it. He walked over to Andy. "What'd I do wrong?"

Andy smiled softly: "You got suckered. But you did it to yourself. You should've boxed me, worked slow, sliced me up. Then when I tired you could have brought in the heavy stuff."

Corbett responded, "Yeah, I agree. But I just couldn't get the memory of those losses out of my mind. It was like a boil."

"Well, man," Andy said, "that boil burst. One word of advice: fight only one fight at a time. You were fighting two old ones and fouling up this one."

Andy patched it up with Sally (I got out of town fast) and they kept succeeding with their love. He worked hard and prospered and ended up owning the foundry. Dick Corbett went on to become a contender but lost the big bout on Tarawa.

Andy and I met occasionally through the years and I became an uncle to their three kids. He came to New York City in 1984 on business and we took in a restaurant and a show. We didn't see any fights. Not for the reason Ray Robinson gives ("It's like a mailman going for a walk") but because the quality has gone out of it. And because the violence has increased precisely as the quality has declined. A while back Ray Lampkin was knocked out by lightweight champion Roberto Duran. Lampkin was out a half-hour and medically it was a touch-and-go business. How did Duran react? "If I had been in normal shape, Lampkin would not have lasted six rounds and he would've gone to the morgue instead of a hospital." A nice guy. Even the dirtiest fighters in the 1930's would never have had such a thought, much less expressed it.

After the show we were walking down Broadway and a big young guy showing off for some friends began to berate Andy for being with a whitey. Andy tried to go around him, the guy blocked him; Andy tried to back away, the dude got in his way again. this one badly wanted to talk: more than talk—he courted injury. I was a bit non-plussed: the guy was black and I didn't know how to handle the race thing. Quick enough, Andy came to my rescue.

"Why do you do this, man?" he asked, slapping down on the guy's left shoulder with his right palm, and "You know you shouldn't" as he slapped his right shoulder with his left just as the fellow started to throw his right. This right-left was double-shock, really a *thwunk*, and I expected the guy's shoelaces to break, because the arches was the region where Andy was focusing. His strings didn't break but his will did and he slunk away favoring two sore shoulders.

"That was a Jack Johnson trick," Andy said. "If the guy had been a little quicker I could've showed you one that Jack learned from mean old Tom Sharkey. As the guy punches, you just chop down on his bicep. With good timing—pop!—the bicep goes dead and you can't use the arm for a week."

After walking away from this encounter, we got to talking about the risks that a known fighter takes with the "fast guns" who try to make a name by quick-hitting or suckering them.

"Dempsey had to have a bodyguard to keep them away," I said ruefully.

"Hell, John," he came back, "that happens to all of them. Joe Louis was once eaten out by a burly truck driver and Joe took it, looking at his feet. A friend asked him later, 'Why didn't you punch him Joe?' Joe laughed, 'If somebody was to insult Caruso, would he sing the guy an aria?'"

Besides showing me class in his boxing and his living, Andy encouraged me to study the history of boxing. He collected the literature and had a complete set of *Ring* since its start in the 1920's. He could argue a point as well as Melvin Belli. We would sit and talk for hours on such recondite matters as:

- How good were the old bareknuckle pugilists?
- Has glove boxing deteriorated since the twenties?
- Who were the greatest boxers of all time?
- Could a wrestler beat a boxer?
- Is boxing ethical or uncivilized and should it be banned?

So all those years while actively boxing, while traveling the world seeking new skills—I studied. What follows is the result. Andy doesn't agree with all of my analysis (no friend would), but, with his memory of the feel of the gloves and the sweat and the thrill of mastery, he ate it up. First we'll look at bareknuckle pugilism and then move on to gloved boxing.

Graeco-Roman Pugilism

Western pugilism started, not with the Greeks as most people believe, but with Middle-Eastern peoples. Near Baghdad, a few decades back, Dr. E. A. Speiser of the University of Pennyslvania

Ancient Pugilists Fighting With the Cestus (from H. Mercurialis, *De Arte Gymnastica*, Venice 1573)

PANCRĂTIVM VOLVTATORIVM

Pancrateists Going All Out (Mercurialis)

John F. Gilbey

found boxing artifacts that date to centuries before the sport was practiced in Greece. Other archaeologists have found traces of pugilism in Egypt that also antedate any evidence of the sport in Greece. Pugilism apparently spread from Egypt via Crete to Greece.

From 900–400 B.C. Grecian pugilism stressed fair play. Soft handwrappings were used for protection. The bout was made part of the Twenty-Third Olympiad in 688 B.C. for which punching bags were used as a training adjunct. As time went on, the soft handwrapping became leather and some of the ethic went out of the matter. The urge to win began to prevail over more genteel considerations.

The evidence suggests that the old pugilists fought from a firm posture. They blocked punches with their left arms but knew little of slipping (moving the head to one side, chiefly against straight punches) and ducking (going under blows, chiefly hooks). Their blows were primarily hammering ones delivered with the right fist.

The pivot punch probably derived from ancient Greece, and was not declared illegal until 1890. This blow was executed by swinging the body—with the arm extended on a horizontal plane either forward or backward—in a complete circle while pivoting on the opposite foot. The centrifugal velocity achieved by this maneuver is enormous. The modern hook is a half pivot, and when it was first introduced many felt it, too, should be barred.

Wrestling and kicking were prohibited in Greek times, and the bouts had no rounds, ending only when one fighter acknowledged defeat. Spartans did not engage in pugilism or the pancration (all-in fighting) because they were never permitted to admit defeat.

The pancration was formally introduced at the Thirty-Third Olympiad and combined boxing and wrestling where no holds were barred. Only biting was forbidden. The Greeks and Romans considered the pancration the ultimate in athletic challenge.

In boxer-versus-wrestler bouts the wrestler invariably wins. In the entire history of the Greek Olympics only two boxing champions, Theagenes and Cleitomachus, won both the boxing and pancration in the same Olympics, while seven wrestling champions added Olympic wins in the pancration. Because the pancration did not permit the use of gloves or cestus (hand girdle), the boxer was at a disadvantage. Without protection or weapon he usually injured his hand on the wrestler's hard parts and was then unceremoniously dumped and defeated by the grappler.

In the first Greek games the fighters came from Greece proper; later they came from all over the empire. After Greece was conquered by Rome, the art degenerated into a Graeco-Roman rivalry of win-at-all-costs until the games were abolished by Emperor Theodosius in 394 A.D.

Pugilism became cruel mauling. Lucillius, writing during the Roman professional period, derides a boxer beaten beyond recognition: "When Odysseus at last, after twenty years, returned home his dog remembered him. But you, Stratophon, after barely four years of fist-fighting, are unknown to the town, let alone to the dogs. If you looked at yourself in the mirror now you would certainly swear: 'That can't be Stratophon.'"

The Romans introduced the cestus and its extension the deadly myrmex "the limb piercer," a bronze spur attached to the cestus, which transformed pugilism from the empty hand to a weaponed form of fighting. Even though the Roman legions spread this decadent pugilism, the basic sport deteriorated and disappeared for eight hundred years from Europe. From 400 A.D. to the eighteenth century there is little documentation of the survival much less the development of Western pugilism. More sanguinary weapons seem to have taken over the field. Fragments recorded in many tales of knights are hardly illuminating from a true martial standpoint. There is one interesting exception: In Sienna, Italy, around 1200 A.D., a priest, later canonized as St. Bernard, came up with the idea of substituting "courteous arms" (fists) for more injurious weapons in the settling of disputes. He even went so far as to teach himself the craft, always stressing the defensive aspects. Throughout his life St. Bernard was able to teach the technique and philosophy of the empty-hand solution to quarrels. To my thinking, it worked out better than the time-honored recourse to knives which usually left one and sometimes both of the disputants

John F. Gilbey

dead.*

They were still boxing at Sienna in the early nineteenth century. According to Stewart Rose's *Letters From Italy* several academies were teaching the art there. At Pisa and Leghorn, however, Rose wrote that the fighters clenched a cylindrical stick, protruding at the end of each fist, to have at each other: the myrmex reincarnated, as always through history. Right up to laser weapons and phony Hollywood ninjas with flying blades. The "triumph" of technology.

British Pugilism

Maurice Maeterlinck, the Belgian dramatist and philosopher, once observed that the fist is the only weapon organically adapted to the sensibilities, the resistance, and the offensive and defensive structure of the human body. A fist, he said, can black an eye but can't get into it because the eye is protected by its bony socket. This kind old gentleman obviously didn't know Fritzie Zivic and Al "Bummy" Davis and never heard of Theagenes of Thasos who reportedly killed over one thousand eight hundred men with his fists back around 500 B.C.

Nor did he know of the pugilists who paraded across British history after the seventeenth century. Except for a vague reference to the fact that soldiers wrestled and boxed at the time of Alfred (849–899), boxing isn't mentioned at all in British literature until the end of the seventeenth century. No doubt pugilism came to

---

*While on the subject of fighting ethics, let me add that another priest deadly with his dukes came along centuries later—Father William Reaney, "The Fighting Chaplain," who introduced boxing in the U.S. Navy during the period roughly from 1892 to 1915. Always willing to fight, once during divine service when a sailor gave him a rough time, he first admonished him from the pulpit, then after the service thrashed him. The sailor turned out to be Tom Sharkey, later a top heavy.

Perfidious Albion with the Roman legions but Tacitus and others are mum about it. We suspect the dirty lineage, though, because the first documented British fighting partook so greatly of the decadent Roman flavor.

Life was hard. Beating someone on the noggin' let you vent some frustration. They'd beat you and if it was dark—to hell with British honor!—they'd kick you or "stop the smoke in your chimney" (strangle you). At the time of the first George (1714–1727) brawling was an hourly occurrence in London with as many as three rings set up at the same time to accommodate the angries. They brawled on the streets, in ale houses, and even in prison (where many of the major bouts were held).

A tragic pugilist of the period was Buckhorse (John Smith). Born amongst thieves who taught their children to pick pockets on coats decked out with bells, Buckhorse was ugly as sin; he could play music on his long flat chin. When short of funds he would let anyone knock him down for a fee. Thus he became a human punching bag and was killed in the street (1730). Other pugilists also came to bad ends. Some turned to crime, more than one "leaping from a leafless tree" (the gallows).

But after a time pugilism took on not only the principles but also some of the flavor of swordplay, becoming a thing of honor best exemplified by the words of an eighteenth century pugilist to his friend: "Tommy, you and I never fell out. And that is why I think we ought to fight."*

In its earliest days prize-fighting had no rules and left no records. Not until James Figg the cudgeller came along (1719) did documentation appear and not until the time of John Broughton, the father of boxing (1732), were the first rules drawn up. Broughton was an excellent swordsman and adapted the tactics of the sword—parry and strike—to the ring where he was preeminent

---

*And may have produced the condition that Lord Chesterfield wrote of: "That silly, sanguine notion . . . that one Englishman can beat three Frenchmen, [which] encourages, and has sometimes enabled, one Englishman, in reality to beat two."

John F. Gilbey

for eighteen years. He introduced gloves as a training aid and also such innovations as stopping and blocking, hitting and retreating. But I think that, like Figg, he was largely a transitional figure in the change from weapons play to pugilism and not himself a great fighter.

The eighteenth century stances may appear to us now as stilted but they served the style of combat then. For one thing, the straight left was a far different blow from what we call a left jab. Pugilists fought to a plan which centered on the left hand extended out front over the left foot. There were few southpaws: I can only think of one great one—Bendigo. The better fighters operated out and back, with the left leg never permitted to step in back of the right leg.

German fencing, incidentally, proved superior to the French and Italian schools for this reason. Because of the integrity of the left foot you were always in a position to deliver a time strike regardless of the circumstances. The French and Italians cavorted back and forth, interchanging front legs, using far too much distance. So British boxing adopted the German fencing stance and developed a straight left strike to go with it. It was not the rat-tat-tat that Ray Robinson used or the playful pecks of an Ali but a bone-jarring smash with considerable body weight behind it. It was part and parcel of a two-pronged long-distance attack that had only a little less power behind it than the right. Its advantages over the right were that it was carried out closer to the opponent and therefore could be delivered quicker and without surrendering balance.

The right, which developed somewhat greater power because of the distance it traveled and the bodyweight it invoked, was used primarily as a cross. But it couldn't be used promiscuously lest it invite that jarring left. So if you hooked or went to a haymaker—as many were tempted when the going got wild—you did so at your own peril. The better boxer held the right fist as a protection against the opponent's left or as a follow-up to what damage his left hand had done. He seldom led with it or swung it wildly.

The head was the chief target, but, because the fist took so much punishment there, it was often easier to go for the body, and pugilists did this almost as a respite. Still, body punching was not much developed early on and even the solar plexus punch had to wait until the time of Bob Fitzsimmons.

Pugilism then was largely linear and long-range. Later, as in-fighting came to the fore, boxers discovered the value of the circle: the rotary motion of hooking punches produced more knockouts because of the swivel effect on the brain.* The relation of pugilism to wrestling also affected strategy. As pugilism developed on its own, the rules prohibited grappling. In the old days you closed with a man not to pummel his midriff but rather to grab him and punch while holding him in chancery—his head under one arm whilst belaboring him with the other—or to grab and throw him.

Never forget that these pugilists were accomplished wrestlers. They found quickly enough that a hard fall often was worth a volley of blows in rendering a man helpless. Moreover, wrestling did not play havoc with their hands.

Bareknuckle bouts resembled the pancration in this respect. Two of the delectable niceties employed were the "suit in chancery" and the cross buttock, a hip throw at the conclusion of which the thrower "accidentally" fell on the man thrown. And more than one boxer imitated the famed Eurydemus (who, it is written, after taking a powerful blow in the mouth swallowed his teeth rather

---

*E. Jokl (1941) regarded the chin uppercut as the most devastating punch, side blows producing a loss of muscle tone but few knockouts. He was concerned with getting the "rebound" effect of the medulla oblongata bouncing back on the occipital bone. He was right—the uppercut on the button will lead to the quickest KO (Jokl also made the interesting observation that a man struck on the carotid artery will collapse straight down, but on a chin will fall backward). However, Jokl underrated the seriousness of side blows. Other researchers have found that most serious brain injuries probably occur where the force of the blow carries a rotational element. This is the swirl effect and it comes mainly from hooks in close. One authority at the turn of the century, boxer F. G. Shaw, saw the danger and wanted the hook outlawed.

John F. Gilbey

than let his opponent know that he'd been hurt) by waiting till he had perpetrated first blood on his antagonist before spitting out blood from his own mouth. Not only from panache but because there was always money bet on first blood. Latin has the saying *pecunia non olet* (money has no smell) which is hooey: here it had the smell and taste of blood.

Eighteenth century pugilism was deficient in several aspects. The stance and strike were so stereotyped that a punch like the elbow smash—though within the rules—was never introduced. For close work the shoulder was never used to good effect even though it wasn't barred until 1947 in the glove era.

Deficient but rough—so rough the sport was prohibited by British courts in 1750. But it remained popular. As it evolved, some of its crueler aspects were eliminated—but not all. From Broughton's informal rules (1743) almost a century passed before the London Prize Ring Rules were introduced in 1838, prohibiting striking below the belt, kicking, and butting. Wrestling was still permitted; hugging on the ropes was barred. On a knockdown the downed fighter got thirty seconds rest plus eight seconds and the help of handlers to come to scratch (the center of the ring). If a man went down without being struck to gain a breather, he forfeited, a rule seldom enforced.

Gouging was prohibited. In the early days it was not unusual for gouging to be performed by twisting the forefinger in a lock of hair near the temple and turning the eye out of the socket with the thumb nail (which was allowed to grow long for the purpose).

I said rough. The longest recorded fight under London Prize Ring Rules was six hours fifteen minutes, the greatest number of rounds 276. Because a round necessarily ended with a knockdown, this means that there were 276 knockdowns in this fight. When a man went down he was given thirty seconds to be ministered to by his handlers ("to give the knee to" was an expression coined from the practice of setting a pugilist down on one of the seconds' knees while rousing or watering him). At the conclusion of this period, the referee would call "time," and the fighters then had eight additional seconds to come to scratch.

In 1866 pugilism was further refined by the Marquis of

Queensberry Rules which mandated gloves and forbade wrestling and clinching and seconds in the ring. Further, they decreed three-minute rounds with one-minute rest intervals and only ten seconds for a downed man to regain his feet.

The demands on endurance were great. Against this test—and the proofs of how good men and true stood up to it—we have the ludicrous Liston and Ali both wanting to quit in their first fight and Liston beating Ali to it.

Some historians discount the trauma of the old prize ring. They cite the fact that barely any deaths occurred and that the pugilists had far fewer fights than boxers nowadays. Actually there were numerous fatalities, though rarely ones in championship fights. And the fact that few of the old timers fought more than a dozen times simply resulted from the inability of their bodies to take any more. Almost every pugilist of note had a hand or two maimed, not once but several times. Bets were made on "first blood" and payoffs invariably occurred in the initial minute. The flow of "claret" was profuse and the conditions of the fighters worsened after the fight when what passed for medical practice then required that they be bled by leeches.

Moreover, the official record doesn't tell the whole story. These fighters fought many unrecorded and unregulated matches out in the rural areas. Take Bob Gregson for example. He had only four prize ring matches and lost them all (to John Gully twice, Tom Cribb, and George Head) but Pierce Egan writes that in Lancashire he fought and won countless unregulated contests where they kicked shins, butted, and gouged to their hearts' content.

Prizefighting imposed a terrific physical strain, and entailed real risk to life. The prizes were fabulous and some of those who survived the slip into brain damage, drink, dissipation, and death ended up with fortunes.

Strangely enough, despite the fights and the grind and the diet—raw eggs to improve the wind and raw beef to make them savage—many pugilists lived to ripe old ages. For example:

Tom Belcher   71
John Broughton 88

Tom Cribb	67
John Gully	81
John Jackson	76
Dan Mendoza	73
Bill Neat	67
Owen Swift	76
Jem Ward	82

. . . but withal a fairly bestial business; tough on both the head and hands. The fragile fist without a cestus out front is poorly designed for sustained hitting. The skin of the knuckles breaks easily and the thin bones making up the hands often fracture. In 1823 Tom Spring won the British championship from Jack Langan but his hand was so severely damaged he never fought again.

And fighting brought out the worst in people. If a pugilist was "asked the question" it meant he was being asked to go in the tank, to cop a fall. When Tommy Griffiths fought Paddy Gill (1850) he was asked and when he refused he was served up a lethal dose of nicotine on a sponge and died in his corner.

Simon Byrne killed Alexander McKay in 1830, was tried for manslaughter, and acquitted. Three years afterward to the very day (June 2) and almost to the very hour Byrne was killed by "Deaf" Burke. Burke later ended up begging on street corners. *Pugilista* said of him: "His qualities were his own, his vices the grafting of his so-called 'betters' in society." The "Little Wonder" (Owen Swift) killed two men and decamped to France where he fought savate experts. He returned later to London where he owned a famous restaurant for twenty-five years before gambling and gout did him in at seventy-six. Bud Taylor, a good American bantam of the 1920s, also killed two men in the ring.

Some Notables

After Broughton, bulk alone prevailed for a long time. Gentleman John Jackson brought some skill into it toward the turn of the eighteenth century. At 6 foot, 196 pounds he probably was pretty

Lord Byron Squaring Off With John Jackson

good. The caveat is because he only fought three times—no one would come to scratch against him. He was a powerful chap who, it is said, could write his name on a wall, with an eighty-pound weight suspended from the little finger of his writing hand. He got the name "Gentleman" because he opened an academy following his retirement at which he trained such notables as Lord Byron. He didn't get the name from the tactics he used against Dan Mendoza which consisted of grabbing poor Mendoza's hair with his right hand and belaboring his head with his left sufficiently to win in ten minutes (1795).

In his bout in 1789 with George Ingleston, Jackson was ahead when he slipped on rainy ground and broke his leg. Jackson offered to fight from a chair (like sailors having their trousers nailed to their sea-chests when they settled differences aboard ship), but Ingleston refused.

Mendoza, a feisty little guy, brought a measure of skill to pugilism chiefly through his footwork, a device to which he had to resort to avoid bulkier opponents. The fighters of the time tended to be brawny. Isaac Perrins, 6'2", 238 pounds, could pick

John F. Gilbey

Humphreys and Mendoza

up a wagon of eight hundred pounds of iron but lost to Tom
Johnson who split his nose as cleanly as with a knife. Another
pugilist, Bill Neate—with his brass knuckles on—could knock
down a bullock. Neate once hit Tom Hickman so hard, Tom stood
transfixed for three seconds, spurted straight up, and then fell over
like a log.

Foreigners also saw some play in Albion. The only Frenchman to participate in the period 1750–1830—and he none too successfully—was one Petit, 6'6" and 220 pounds, the Carnera of his day. A decade later an American behemoth arrived. At 6'10", 322 pounds Charlie Freeman could lift 1,500 pounds from the ground, run like the wind, and do somersaults. There was only one thing he couldn't do—fight. Severely beaten by William Perry in 1842, Freeman died three years later.

The man who produced the greatest change in British tactics was Jem Belcher, Champion at only seventeen (1798–1809), he used both hands and coupled his fist work with excellent wrestling tactics and revolutionary footwork (he was relatively small, never scaling over 170 pounds). Many claim that the man from Bristol, despite his weight, was the best of the bareknuckle tradition.

Others say no, that Henry Pearce ("The Game Chicken") who beat Belcher was the better man. But though Pearce (5'9", 182 lbs.) has to be adjudged in the top rank of his time (he retired undefeated), he lacked Belcher's all-around ability. His win, incidentally, came after Belcher had been idle two years and blinded in one eye in an accident. Pearce was the only pugilist to go undefeated, but in the ultimate match against the grim reaper he lost to the effects of too much wine and too many women, dying at thirty-two.

And there was little Dutch Sam, the lightweight who some say had the hardest punch in history.* Trained by John Jackson, during the period 1805–14 Sam, who is credited with having invented the uppercut, fought ten bouts and won them all. He claimed to have escaped the run of matches without suffering a black eye himself. He once told Henry Pearce that he, Pearce,

---

*If we had a machine that would measure striking power and if we could retroactively gauge these old timers and compare them with the recent crop, would that prove anything? Sure. It would prove whether the pugilists as a class punched harder than the boxers. But the punch is only one factor; hence the machine could not tell us who would prevail in the classic "square of hemp and timber."

John F. Gilbey

couldn't beat him in fifteen minutes. Pearce, the then heavyweight champion, didn't try.

Sam was an iron man with the kick of a stallion. Undefeated he was—but only in the ring. In training for a fight in 1805 he got to quarreling in the street with a butcher named James Brown. They came to blows. During a pause in the proceedings in which the butcher was having the best of it, one of Sam's friends told the butcher the name of the man with whom he was brawling. "Be he the devil," the butcher said, "I'll bang him well now that I am at it." And he did. (In fairness to Sam who weighed only 130 pounds, he may have been giving away a lot of weight.)

The terrible Bendigo beat Ben Caunt in ninety-three rounds in a match that saw the equivalent of a million dollars change hands. Bendigo, who was jailed twenty-eight times for disturbing the peace, later found religion and became an evangelist. He was another who claimed to have come through his battles unscathed with no black eyes or other injuries. Maybe so. But this doesn't jibe with eyewitnesses who said that as an evangelist he was a poor speaker because all his front teeth had been knocked out (he claimed to have lost a tooth playing football and broken a kneecap somersaulting—but that doesn't account for the other teeth).

A word on the bout between the British champion Tom Sayers and the American champion John Heenan. Recalled as the greatest of all time, it may have waxed grand in the memory. It went for two hours and a half to a draw. Sayers had the best of the early going and at one point hit Heenan in the ribs, the blow sounding, according to the *Times* correspondent, "all over the meadow as if a box had been smashed in." At the end, when Sayers, fighting gamely with but one hand, was being strangled on the ropes (a clear violation of the rules), his backers cut the strands, and the fight was called off.

A great fight it may have been but neither fighter himself was all that great. Sayers was smallish (153 pounds) with almost no biceps (but, Wilkie Collins observed, beautifully developed triceps) and Heenan never won a big fight in his life. John Morrissey beat him in America and would give him a return go only on condition he beat Sayers. Tom King beat him following the Sayers match. Heenan then gave up fistics, married Adah Isaacs Menken, a famous actress, and went into politics.

Two national heroes figured in the bareknuckle fighting of this era. To the Irish, Daniel Donnelly is the greatest fighter of all time. Although he was undefeated, he met no one of note. He shines for me because of his memorable line: "I will give you my opinion as to what I think necessary to be done on such occasions. First of all you must take off your shirt."

On the English side, John Shaw beat everyone in Nottingham including two professionals, Burrows and Ned Painter. Negotiations for a fight between him and Tom Cribb (the champion) were in progress when Shaw fell at Waterloo in 1815 after dispatching ten or so of Napoleon's best. He is enshrined in British memory (Sir Walter Scott eulogized him) as a warrior saint on a level with mythical kings of the past.

The Teachers

Among the famed nineteenth-century teachers were John Jackson, Captain Barclay (Allardyce), George Head, and Jem Mace. Jackson we have spoken of above. Barclay was reckoned a good, if bad-tempered, fighter and a hard taskmaster as a trainer. When he trained Tom Cribb for his epic match with the negro Molineaux, he forced Tom to walk sixty miles before he would feed him. Barclay could also be devious. He kept a pair of trick gloves in his gym, appropriately weighted with lead, with which he would belabor the unwary. Once Molineaux came in for a workout and, not realizing it, put on Barclay's gloves. Barclay couldn't tell the black the secret and so put on a pair of regular gloves and had at it. Fittingly, Molineaux broke one of Barclay's ribs during the first set-to.

George Head was a better pugilist and teacher. Well educated, he wrote a treatise of boxing and even tried his hand at poetry. As a boxer he was never defeated and was the most scientific purveyor of the science in the early 1800s. In prison he beat

John F. Gilbey

Tom Reynolds with and without gloves and also demolished Bob Gregson. Outside prison he accepted all comers and prevailed.

But the best teacher may also have been the best fighter of the pugilistic era: Jem Mace. The only thing against the gypsy was his weight, seldom more than 150 pounds. Starting in a public boxing booth by taking on all comers, he eventually won the championship (1861). Because of his great skill, he became known as the father of modern scientific boxing. He fought bareknuckle and with gloves. When reform elements threatened the sport locally, he went to America and Australia, beating the champions there. He taught the great Larry Foley in Australia, and Foley passed the science on to such boxers as Box Fitzsimmons, Peter Jackson, Frank Slavin, and Young Griffo.

The Aussie is leather tough whether alone or with someone (the Irish, such stalwarts individually, crumble when in a crowd). I remember serving with the Aussies in World War II in the Pacific and they made our Marines look like girls. They were big in a fighting way, even the small ones, and brought to mind those that John Masefield, the poet, saw on Gallipoli: "They walked and looked like the kings in old poems."

Down under, Mace was once asked to curb a local terror. "Are you spoiling for a fight, Murphy, this morning?" asked the man's employer. "Well to tell yer the truth soir, I'm agitting' toired o'peace and quoitness, and I'd loike to 'ave a foight'," the toughie responded. So he squared off with Mace and was drubbed severely.

After his sojourn in the Antipodes, Mace returned to England and continued teaching and fighting. He actually fought four times when he was past sixty. Sadly, he died broke in 1910 after being champion of two hemispheres, doing the thing he started at: traveling with a boxing booth. Maybe that is the fitting way for a gypsy.

Mace didn't invent the boxing booth, even though he spent a good part of his life in one. Actually, the documents describing the booth date back quite a bit earlier. Samuel Johnson's uncle, Andrew,* opened one of the first ones in London. The booth or

---

*Blood tells. Here is the nephew speaking: "Every man has a right to

Jem Mace, Perhaps the Best of the Pugilists

John F. Gilbey

tent boxer was common throughout the world at the turn of the century; in England alone over eighty booths flourished. Figg, Mace, Jimmy Wilde, Tommy Farr, and many others got started by taking on as many as thirty-two comers a day. In the 1950s only twelve booths were left in Britain. Ron Taylor had one. And he also had an estimable grandma. "She used to challenge all comers. She wore chest protectors but never needed 'em. Nobody she ever went up against could ever come close to hitting her."

Modern Boxing

The knockout so much in evidence after 1900 was a rarity in the old days. Part of the reason lay in the style of fighting. Under London Prize Ring Rules the straight left kept a man at bay, or at least cautious. But later with the introduction of the hook and the quick KO many boxers risked getting in close to use the new device in spite of the left, which now, diluted by gloves,* was no longer the danger it had been once.

Of course the duration of counts makes the KO itself a mere technicality in comparing eras. A hit to the "mark" (solar plexus) paralyzes the diaphragm and produces a lot of pain, but it doesn't cause unconsciousness or lasting injury. In boxing it makes for a

---

utter what he thinks truth, and every other man has a right to knock him down for it."

* The gloves invented by Broughton for training purposes ("mufflers") were probably ten ounces; when they came into ring use under the Marquess of Queensberry Rules (1864) they were five ounces (although many fights in the period 1885–92 were with two-ouncers). The Corbett-Sullivan fight was with five-ounce gloves. Now the minimum is set at eight ounces. Mouth guards were used by ancient Hellenic boxers, but not in the modern era until 1912. Much later, the Taylor foulproof cup was introduced to protect the genitals.

KO, but in pugilism the victim usually was well enough to continue after his thirty-eight seconds. Although head punches could produce KO's, many pugilists shook off the effects of even these in the allotted span, while a boxer could not recover in ten seconds. The extra twenty-plus seconds is crucial since the effect of many KO's is temporary and, after that, the recovery rate is relatively rapid.

The chief name from the transitional period between pugilism and modern boxing was John L. Sullivan, 5'10", 190 pounds. Sullivan fought seventy-five times, winning sixteen by KO, three by decision, and was knocked out once—by Corbett. He started his athletic career in baseball and then became a wrestler; he probably could have functioned fine in pugilism. The "probably" is because he fought only one man of note bareknuckled. That was Jake Kilrain, whom he fouled in the forty-fifth round by stomping on him—a clear violation of the rules. But he didn't foul out, probably because Kilrain had provoked him into it by falling down repeatedly without being struck so as to gain the thirty-eight second respite—itself a violation of the rules. Sullivan finally won in the seventy-fifth. Interestingly, prize-fighting was illegal in America until the turn of the century and both Sullivan and Kilrain spent time in the pokey after their 1889 fight.

Sullivan fathered the KO but, as we have seen, he was aided substantially by the new rule. The ratio of knockouts to total fights is a datum that tells something of a man's punching power—but not everything. If you look at the KO ratio of some of the heavyweight greats it will surprise you.

Sullivan (!)	21%
Corbett	27%
Johnson	39%
Langford	39%
Wills	44%
Carpentier	48%
Tunney	54%
Fitzsimmons	56%
Sharkey	68%
Jeffries	69%

John F. Gilbey

John L. Sullivan

The list is surprising in that powerful John L. scored the least percentage of KO's—less even than the consumate boxer, Corbett—and Tunney, supposedly a light hitter, had one of the highest ratios. One explanation has to do with the role of boxing in American life in different eras: Sullivan fought a lot of no-decision affairs (forty-one)—as did Langford and Johnson—in which they "carried" opponents for entertainment's sake. Sullivan barnstormed and won eighty-four of eighty-five bouts within four rounds, only having to pay up the $1,000 "lasting" fee once. These matches never got into the record books. Peter Maher, who reputedly had the strongest right hand of any heavy in history, only scored forty percent, and Joe Choynski who Jeffries and several others said hit them the hardest, only thirty-one percent. But Joe never scaled over 165 pounds and if weight is figured into the equation it would make him a helluva slugger.

Sullivan and Corbett headed the list of boxers who fought in bars and barges and carnivals. Corbett was such a polished boxer that he offered $200 to anyone who could stay with him in exhibitions. Sullivan, who did most of his training and fighting in taverns—he once drank six quarts of whiskey in five hours!—made similar offers and only one man ever collected by lasting the stipulated time. Joe Walcott and George Dixon also took all challengers for little or no money while they sharpened their wares and legitimized the new sport. At the same time Jem Mace, Jem Driscoll, Joe Bowker, Pedlar Palmer, and Jimmy Wilde were doing the same thing in England and elsewhere.

We've kicked it off with Sullivan. How to continue in a sport on which reams have been written? I can't possibly do all the great ones justice, and it would take a massive volume whether I were to attempt it chronologically or alphabetically, so let me jump in where angels fear to tread by going the qualitative route. Because slicing it down to the best in each division is so difficult, let me name the top two in each and then digress a bit on my choices. Here they are.

> Heavyweight: Jack Johnson and Joe Louis
> Light-heavyweight: Sam Langford and Georges Carpentier
> Middleweight: Stanley Ketchel and Harry Greb
> Welterweight: Joe Walcott and the Dixie Kid
> Lightweight: Joe Gans and Benny Leonard
> Featherweight: Terry McGovern and Young Griffo
> Bantamweight: George Dixon and Pete Herman
> Flyweight: Jimmy Wilde and Pancho Villa

The best pound-for-pound? Easy—Jimmy Wilde, followed by Gans, Dixon, and Walcott.

34   *John F. Gilbey*

The Heavyweights

Jack Johnson was by all odds the greatest heavy of the glove era. He was an exceptional boxer and could take you out with either hand. He toyed with Jim Jeffries (1910), Frank Moran,* and other heavies, the only blemish being his KO loss to Jess Willard in the twenty-sixth round in Havana in 1915, but this was obviously a tank job to appease the racists of the time. Johnson himself gives the lie to the KO in the photograph where he lies with his arm raised to shield his eyes from the sun. The other proof is in Willard's clear inability to fight. Willard was big but too awkward ever to cope with Johnson in a real fight. He was so bad that when he fought Joe Cox in Springfield, Missouri, he actually hid behind the referee a la Charlie Chaplin in "City Lights."

Uncle Joe Woodman who managed Sam Langford didn't think the accolade of greatest should go to Jack Dempsey. He gave the palm to Johnson, the big cat ("He could stand on a foot-square handkerchief and you couldn't touch a hair of his head.") Damon Runyan and Ace Hudkins, writer and boxer, respectively, agreed. Dempsey himself said the farther back you went the tougher they were—and Johnson was the toughest of the old timers: "He was all elbows and arms, the greatest catcher of punches who ever lived. Johnson could uppercut moving backward and could cut to the body off a jaw feint and hook off a jab better than any heavyweight who ever lived."

Johnson knew Nelson Algren's two primary rules for surviving in the ring: (1) never pull your head back from a butt (otherwise he'll butt you back), and (2) always follow a dirty blow with a clean one. Not that he was a dirty fighter: he didn't have to

---

*Frank Moran, an aspiring heavy, had a good right punch that he nicknamed "Mary Ann." But that was all he had. And it wasn't enough. It was just too easy to protect against this one weapon. So, though he had two chances at the crown, Frank lost them both. The moral: you have to have more than one weapon to last in this race.

Jack Johnson   Joe Louis

be—he was too good a clean fighter. But he was a survivor and could return whatever—clean or dirty—came his way.

Joe Louis rose from the Alabama cotton fields and was a stylistic contrast to Johnson. He couldn't catch an opponent's fists the way Jack could, but he didn't need to. He'd shuffle in, always measuring, and, like Gans, wait for you to make a mistake. Or he could force the fight, as he did against Schmeling in their second match (1938). He countered better than anyone except possibly Johnson. His one big defect: he never learned to handle a short right hand. It is ironic that sportswriters thought he was acting out of a combination of bravery and revenge in bombing Schmeling out in the first round of their second go. Add *fear* to that. Joe never learned to handle Schmeling's short chopping right in training camp. The only way to thwart it was to go out blazing, a thing Louis never did before or after. The tactic worked, so well in fact that he should have used it more often. He was essentially a conservative plodding battler. But his countering was exquisite, and it more than compensated.

John F. Gilbey

Close on the heels of these two was Peter Jackson, followed, further back, by Gene Tunney. In a dream match Louis, the inimitable counter puncher, would have made short work of Dempsey who had trouble with counter punchers. For the same reason Marciano would have fallen if matched with the bomber at his prime.

Jack Johnson said that Peter Jackson could have beaten Louis. Perhaps. Peter Jackson could do almost anything. More telling than Johnson's judgment though is that of Corbett who said Jackson was the greatest he ever saw, and died talking of his sixty-one round draw with Jackson in 1891. Jackson was schooled by Larry Foley at his famous White House Inn in Australia. In his prime (1888–92) he went undefeated and even Sullivan refused to come to scratch against him.

Corbett's judgment is important because he KO'd such toughies as Sullivan, Choynski, Mitchell, and Kid McCoy (while losing to Jeffries, Fitzsimmons, and Tom Sharkey). And—though he tried to erase it from his memory later in life—Corbett would never face Jackson again.

Jackson was so good that in some exhibitions he wasn't permitted to use his right hand. Thus by the time he reached his peak, he had a left that could do everything but talk—and even that whispered loud. He thus was able to translate pugilism to modern boxing and excel at both.

In 1892 the dream match took place in London; Peter Jackson versus Frank Slavin.* Both were over six foot and approaching two hundred pounds, both were Aussies, one black, one white. Undaunted by Slavin's evil eye (said to be nearly as bad as Sullivan's which in turn made Liston's or Ali's look like a little girl trying to decide on which candy to buy), Jackson rode out Slavin's

---

*Interestingly, at one point Slavin was almost drawn into a match with a *judoka* in Japan. If memory serves, he was to face Iizuka, later tenth grade black belt. The arrangement fell through, however. It would have been something to see. Slavin, besides being an excellent boxer, was an accomplished grappler.

best blows and was able to prevail in the twelfth. This was the real "Gentleman Jackson:" when the referee refused to stop the carnage, Jackson said, "Well, I'm sorry, Frank" and delivered the *coup de grace*. For his part, Frank, after he was brought around, said sadly: "They'll never believe it in Australia."

What finally did Jackson in was his lack of success in inducing whites to face him. You have to keep this in mind whenever you evaluate any black boxer. Blacks met a color bar up through the 1920s. Jackson came to the U.S. and no one would fight him: Sullivan et. al. looked the other way. George Dixon and Joe Walcott never got the fights they desired. Nor did Langford, Jeannette, McVey, Willis, and so many others. Racism squelched them and, over time, wore down their abilities by forcing them to fight among themselves. Look at the multiple fights these craftsmen had with each other and you'll conclude that it was criminal.

Hence, when a black met a white of note, he had to make accommodations of one sort or another—weight, age, and so on. When Jackson finally met Jeffries in 1898 he had been acting for five years in such shows as "Uncle Tom's Cabin." Eaten up by drink and disgust, this shell of a man fell in three.

The fourth spot goes to Tunney. Long before he met Dempsey in 1926, he was highly rated. He won the lightheavy crown in 1922 and was beaten only once in seventy-six bouts, and that by Harry Greb. Grantland Rice wrote, "Greb handled him like a butcher hammering a swiss steak." In their subsequent four meetings Tunney beat Greb, and also TKO'd Carpentier and Tom Gibbons. Most people think he squeaked by Dempsey. Wrong. Dempsey won only one round in the two fights. Gene retired rich before his peak and for this reason he is not as highly valued, but he should be. He did it all with bad hands and motivation. He wasn't fooled by the raging crowd, terming its gore lust "The blood-thirsty yap of the mob."

Why isn't Sullivan* up there? Simply because he doesn't

---

* Although I don't rate him that high as a boxer, I rather like Sullivan for his sage advice to youth: "Don't get the fool notion in your head that you ought to go to college. Keep out of politics and learn to box."

John F. Gilbey

belong. Asked once to rate Sullivan against Dempsey, Jack Mc-
Auliffe, who seconded Sullivan against Corbett at New Orleans,
said: "It would have been heart-breaking in its suddenness. Three
punches. John would have landed the first punch to the chin, a
right, and Dempsey the next two, a right to the heart and a left
to the jaw. That would be all."

The Light Heavyweights

Jack Dempsey said that Sam Langford was the greatest fighter
ever. If Jack was wrong, it wasn't by much. Sam Langford boxed
from 1902 to 1923 by which time half-blind, he had to be steered
to the ring and pointed at his opponent. Piloted by the great Joe
Woodman, Sam had arms so long he could scratch his ankles without bending his knees, fast hands, and extraordinary strength. He
fought lights to heavies in 640 bouts, only three hundred or so
recorded. He was so good he only got to go with blacks: he fought
Harry Wills twenty-two times (giving away forty pounds); Sam
McVey fifteen times; Joe Jeannette fourteen times. And won most
of them.

Langford (at 158 lbs.) fought Jack Johnson (185 lbs.) in 1906
and there have been stories for years that he gave Johnson so much
trouble that Johnson would never fight him again. The fact is that
Langford lost handily to the bigger man, an opponent who not
only had a considerable weight advantage on him but also just
happened to be the classic boxer of all time. A loss to Johnson certainly cannot dim the luster of the "Boston Tar Baby."

Late in life, blind and destitute, he stayed in his tiny room
on a Harlem diet ("When I'm hungry and I ain't got the price
of a feed, I drink a glass of water and pick my teeth. Then I use
my imagination"). He died beautifully, never complaining about
the color bar, the dollars that disappeared, and the fickle, forget-
ful public.

Carpentier, like Tunney, was far better than many realize.
He lost to Dempsey and Tunney when he was past his prime after

George Carpentier   **Sam Langford**

fighting twenty years. He began his career with savate rules under
Francois Deschamps in 1906. With a smooth one-two and one
of the solidest rights ever, he was rudely initiated at seventeen
by the Dixie Kid but came on to beat middles Klaus and Papke.
At 155 pounds he even took on heavies successfully—and kept his
classic features together in the bargain. In 1913 he knocked out
Bombardier Wells in the first round to take the heavyweight championship of Europe. After seeing service in World War I he beat
Joe Beckett, the British champ, in the first round. Of this fight,
George Bernard Shaw wrote, "It was like Charles XII of Sweden
had come striding along in a Japanese dressing gown." Later,
asked about Beckett, Carpentier said: "I don't know: I never met
the man." It can happen. Nelson Algren once told Hemingway

John F. Gilbey

about Nate Bolden whipping Zale twice in one month before World War II. After the war, Algren got into a cab in Chicago and there was Bolden driving. Algren says, "I saw you beat Zale," to which Bolden responds, "Oh, which one was he?" (It wasn't that Bolden was punchy: he just didn't remember the names of the men he fought.)

The Middleweights

Stan Ketchel was the greatest middle of the glove era. His KO percentage was seventy-five percent and he even knocked Jack Johnson down.* He knocked out the first thirty-five of thirty-nine men he faced. Among those he tagged: Billy Papke, Mike Sullivan, Willie Lewis, and Philadelphia Jack O'Brien (O'Brien, an exceptional fighter himself, called Ketchel, "a tumultuously ferocious person").

In his early days in a Colorado mining town, Ketchel once kayoed six heavyweights one after the other. He carried one chap so the man could last and use the money to buy a violin for his son—the closest Ketchel probably ever got to culture, for the boy turned out to be Fritz Kreisler, the greatest violinist in the world. He ended his days eating with a gun in his lap and was shot from behind at twenty-three by a hired man with whose girlfriend he had been dallying. The last words on Ketchel belong to his one-time manager, Wilson Mizner, "I think of him as a laugh, a pair of shoulders, and a great heart."

Harry Greb lost only seven fights in nearly three hundred, beating every ranking middle (Johnny Wilson, from whom he won the title in 1923, Mickey Walker, and Tiger Flowers) and was the only man to beat Tunney. Greb invented the windmill/swarm

---

*Up Jack got, though, and lowered Stan with a punch that left a couple of Stan's teeth imbedded in Jack's glove. *Apropros* this hazard, the Hoosier humorist, Kin Hubbard, once wrote: "I'll bet th' hardest thing 'bout prize fightin' is pickin' up yer teeth with a boxin' glove on."

Stan Ketchel   Harry Greb

style copied later by Henry Armstrong and Jackie Kid Berg. Mc-
Govern, Ketchel, Dempsey, and Marciano were all wade-in types,
but they would breathe occasionally and could box when occasion
demanded.

Because it couples power and speed, the middleweight division traditionally has been the one packed with most action. The
best boxing series I ever saw was the war between Tony Zale and
Rocky Graziano. In 1946 they met the first time, Zale the betting underdog. But Zale took the hooker in the sixth round. The
next year Graziano did it to him also in the sixth round after Zale
had won five straight bouts by KO. Then in 1948 Zale turned
the tables on Graziano in the torrid third match by dumping him

in the third. Never before or since have two men with such disparate styles—Zale the balanced boxer and puncher, Graziano the winger—put on such a sizzling series.

But there were many great middles. Though Ketchel heads the list, Greb gets pressure from fighters like Les Darcy, Kid McCoy, and Ray Robinson.

Les Darcy was an exceptional middle. A dream match between Darcy and Ketchel would be worth poling down the River Styx to see. After beating everyone in his native Australia, he came to America in 1917, only to be hounded by our sportswriters and accused of dodging the draft. To show his good faith, he joined the Tennessee National Guard but the harassment proved too much and he died of a mental breakdown in 1917, only twenty-one years of age. He notched twenty KO's in thirty-nine fights, losing only three decisions early in his abbreviated career. He beat such celebrated Americans as George Chip, Jeff Smith, Jimmy Clabby, and Eddie McGoorty.

Kid McCoy (Norman Selby) had a consummate corkscrew, executed by turning his left standing fist a quarter rotation or so onto the horizontal plane as it stuck. He began pushing gloves in 1891 and went twenty-five years, the last twelve undefeated. He handled those in his own weight easily—he KO'd the fine Tommy Ryan in the fifteenth round of their welter title match (1906)—but had trouble with bigger boys. Tom Sharkey and Jim Corbett outgunned him with superior weight. After leaving the ring, McCoy made a million dollars in the movies but, sadly, died a suicide in 1940. He once knocked out a chap in a tavern who claimed to be him, then remarking, "That is the real McCoy," thus coining a phrase still used.

Sugar Ray Robinson was handsome and smooth as silk in the ring with a KO percentage of over fifty percent. He deserved and got a good press and yet I think Tony Zale and Marcel Cerdan were almost in his class.

Zale was a moxie boxer and hard as nails. Small wonder they called him the man of iron. It was no use hitting him in the body: he could take anything there—and counter it to boot. Melio Bettina kidney-punched Zale throughout one fight and he could do nothing to prevent it. Later in the gym he learned to jerk his elbow into the wrist of the kidney-punching fist at the right moment without dropping his guard. This sharp crack can break a wrist. Zale never worried about the kidney punch again. He was a workhorse and was trained to perfection by Johnnie Coulon, the former bantam champ.

Today a fighter can take a divisional crown in a pittance of bouts over a few years. Go back and look at the work Zale did to earn his middle title. He won the Indiana Golden Gloves in 1931 at age eighteen. The next year he was Golden Glove runner-up in Chicago. After ninety-five fights he turned pro in 1934. Seven years and seventy-two fights later he won the middle title.

The Frenchman, Marcel Cerdan, had the potential for greatness. True, Jake Lamotta beat him, but only after Cerdan had injured a shoulder in the first round. His home life was chaotic too, involved as he was with that little songbird, Edith Piaf, but I think this one with a lethal left hook that travelled only a few inches would have gone high if his plane hadn't fallen out of the sky.

The Welterweights

Joe Walcott was a truly great boxer. A champion wrestler before he tackled boxing, Joe had 150 *official* fights and *twice* that number in carnivals. His record appears inconsistent at first glance but keep in mind he fought twenty-one years, usually giving away poundage. And, with the color bar, he occasionally had to accommodate whites. He beat Sam Langford and Joe Gans and knocked out Joe Choynski, one of the best heavies in the world. That sentence says it all.

Right up there with Walcott as a welter was the terrific Dixie Kid (Aaron Brown). The Kid was one of the deadliest ringmen ever and a helluva character outside the ring. In 122 fights he knocked out a whopping fifty-one percent of his opponents. He drew with Walcott once and beat him on a foul in another bout. He also beat Carpentier, Clabby, and others of note but fell victim to the heavier Langford twice. He was astute at appearing

Joe Walcott

Aaron Brown, The Dixie Kid

out on his feet, drawing an opponent in, and then annihilating him. He was deported from London in 1914 and went to Spain where he was accused of selling false information to both the British and the Germans—which got him deported from Spain. An unprecedented record in diplomatic annals. As innovative out of the ring as in, he is credited with inventing the zip fastener! This guy deserves a full-fledged volume all to himself.

Not too far back is Jack Britton who fought from 1905 to 1930. Jack was a honey. He beat Leonard but lost to Mickey Walker on a decision in 1922 as much to age as to Walker. He fought Ted "Kid" Lewis twenty times and was involved in a record 177 no-

John F. Gilbey

decision goes, most of which he actually won. Britton was one of the best of all time at ducking and slipping to avoid using his arms for blocking.

Some boxers never quit. Whitey Bimstein once told of the death of Frankie Jerome, a boxer he was seconding at Madison Square Garden: "He died in my arms, slipping punches."

The Lightweights

Jack McAuliffe was the first lightweight champ to retire undefeated (1914). Benny Leonard was the next. Who was the best lightweight of all time? Neither one. Joe Gans, from out of the Baltimore fish markets. He knocked out the first man he ever faced (1891) and ran up a string of fifty-six straight through eight years when George "Elbows" McFadden stopped him in the twenty-third round ("His elbows had eyes of their own"). After winning the next eleven, he lost via KO to Frank Erne and Terry McGovern in 1900. He then won nineteen straight and knocked out Erne for the title. He held the title for six years, taking on such men as Battling Nelson, Joe Walcott, and Jimmy Britt, but finally lost to Nelson on a knockout in 1908.

Gans died in an insane asylum in 1951 and the obit read simply: "He leaves a sister." A bit inadequate for one who had every move, who could take it and shell it out. Not a cute fighter, he would shuffle around, tailing, take what came, most of it on his arms, and then counter with his potent right. He was good with his elbows—a technique perhaps picked up from McFadden. He used elbows expertly in blocking, and if he missed a cross wasn't averse to thwacking the elbow in as a finisher, a tactic still seen in Thai Boxing rings.

I rank Benny Leonard close to Joe Gans. After being knocked out in his first fight (with Mickey Finnegan in 1911), he went undefeated as a lightweight and welter until Jimmy McLarnin KO'd him in 1932, seven years after he'd retired as lightweight champ. Leonard was marvelous and his hair seldom got mussed. But he could also hit, having a KO percentage of thirty-two percent. He

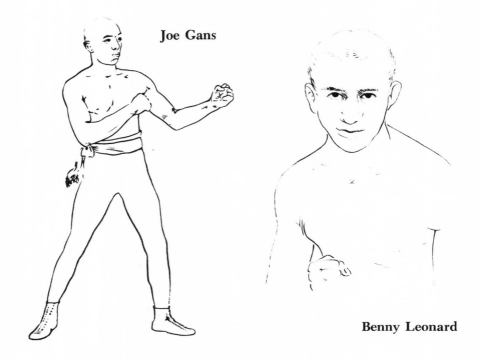

Joe Gans

Benny Leonard

liked boxing and thought it refined a man. It is just as well he never met Battling Nelson who actually kicked Joe Gans in the forty-second round of their match, thereby losing on a foul.

A slight amendment. In 1922, lacking competition, Leonard moved up to the welter class to tangle with Jack Britton. As usually happens, weight told and Britton was too much for him. Leonard went back to the lightweights. It is said that Papa used this fight as background for his short story "Fifty Grand." He left out one anecdote: after the fight Britton reportedly said that Leonard was the smartest man to ever lace on gloves, but the only trouble was that while Leonard was thinking, he, Britton, was beating the devil out of him.

Jimmy Britt lightweight champ (1904) loved to tell how tough his family was. According to him, there was one street in San Francisco, the meanest street in the world. As police walked down it they would be joined by others. The farther you went down the street, the rougher the houses became. "We lived," Jimmy said, "in the last house." Britt was tough in a tough era. He stopped

George "Kid" Lavigne—a feat few others could pull off. But he couldn't have done it earlier: Lavigne's high living had softened him by the time they squared off.

Better than Britt was Packey McFarland who never lost a bout after being KO'd in his first year (1904), going twelve years with a KO record of forty-five percent. The only thing holding him down in the rankings was the lack of quality in his opposition.

Joe Benjamin was a better than average lightweight. One night after he retired he was sitting in a San Francisco tavern and a toxic stranger laid into him.

"I saw Benny Leonard beat you in Frisco."

"Right."

"I saw you lose to Lew Tendler in Reno."

"Yep."

"I also saw Willie Ritchie beat you."

Joe looked evenly at the man and said: "Then you've never seen me win a fight. Well—you will now."

The lesson here is never to talk about lost battles to old fighters. Most get tougher as their memories get weaker and they'll swear that they got jobbed out of the decision in some way. Even if they accept it, they're not going to like you bringing up unpleasant memories.

The Featherweights

"Terrible" Terry McGovern won the bantam championship by knocking out Pedlar Palmer* in the first round (1899) and the next

---

*Palmer had been undefeated since 1891. A bit erratic—when he was good he was very good. He beat George Dixon three out of five times. An interesting aside: England didn't register its fighters, but it was still tough on those using their talents outside the ring. Palmer once got seven years' servitude for knocking out a man he claimed had insulted a lady in a public place. He went off to the pokey despite what would seem to be a reasonable excuse. The irony of this case, though, is that Palmer was known as a tricky battler but with no punch.

Albert Griffiths (Young Griffo)

year KO'd the great George Dixon for the feather crown, then decisioned him, and KO'd Frank Erne and Joe Gans. The next year he KO'd the hard-hitting Aurelio Herrera. He was one of the finest body punchers who ever lived. The only blemishes in his record were two KO losses to Young Corbett, a natural lightweight.

Right with McGovern is the greatest defensive genius Western boxing has had, Young Griffo (Albert Giffiths) from down under.

John F. Gilbey

Terry McGovern

A lot of conversation has been made about how fancy Young Griffo was, the most adroit critter ever to enter the squared circle. He was as slippery as spaghetti in a discount Italian joint. But his critics claim he was heavily marked, so that someone must have been hitting him. On the other hand, Stan Ketchel who wouldn't move his head for any man was relatively unscarred. We know that Ketchel was hit far more than Griffo and so the explanation is simply that some men don't show the ravages of the ring to the same extent that others do.

"If grandma had wheels she'd be a wheelbarrow" goes the old saw and the contingent "ifs" in boxing produce enduring young delight among old fans. If Young Griffo had had a punch he'd been the greatest pound-for-pound fighter of all time (but, old shoe, if he'd planted his feet to get more sock into his fists he would've had to sacrifice some of his phantom defensive wares). Okay then, try this. If Griffo had ever been sober he would have been the greatest. Maybe. It is certainly true that no one ever saw him sober. Drunk, he could stand on a handkerchief and no one could touch him. And catch a fly between his thumb and index finger. And win most of his 107 bouts, beating the best in the division. He easily beat Jack McAuliffe in 1894 but got jobbed out of the decision—one of the worst in the annals of boxing. And this at ten pounds under McAuliffe's bodyweight.

Critics say Griffo was a light puncher. Right. And that he lost to Dixon, Lavigne, and Gans. Correct, but who didn't? That's quite a threesome. Considering the fact that Griffo never trained and subsisted almost entirely on alcohol,* I think he has to go down as a peerless feather.

Hard on the heels of McGovern and Griffo were Jem Driscoll and Willie Pep. From Wales, Driscoll was a fine feather who stopped George Dixon and Joe Bowker, topped Abe Attell, and was only beaten once (in his last fight, eighteen years after he started) in seventy-one bouts in which his KO percentage was thirty-eight percent. He was poetry as a fighter, but never was given a title shot.

Willie Pep would have been great in any period. From his first pro go in 1940 he won 136 fights, losing only one decision, until he lost to Sandy Saddler in 1948. He had a splendid array of punches and could take a good wallop.

---

* Another boxer with a booze problem was Lew Jenkins, lightweight champion in 1940. Lew fell down getting into the ring once from the effects of liquor and the referee had to drag him to his stool. Drunk or sober, he won most of his matches.

John F. Gilbey

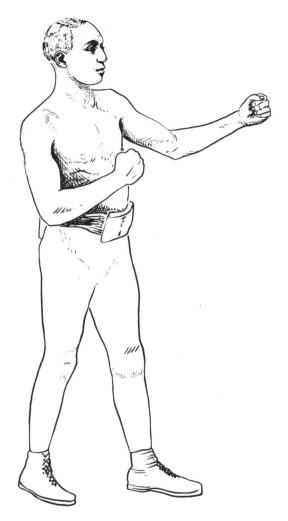

George Dixon

The Bantamweights

At bantam there are only George Dixon ("Little Chocolate") and Pete Herman (Gulotta). A finer pair never shuffled their feet in the resin box.

George Dixon lost on twenty-one decisions and four knock-outs, but, considering the number of his bouts (over eight hundred,

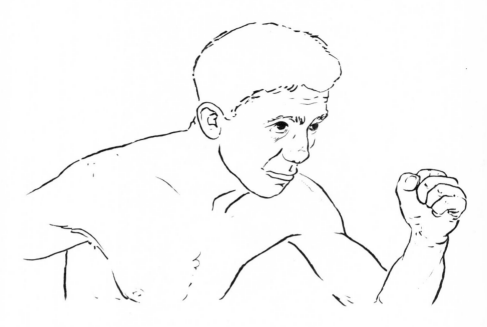

Pete Herman

most of them barnstorming), tenure (twenty years), and the fact
that he often fought feathers or heavier, I'll get little argument
on him. Not a particularly heavy hitter, he was merely a consummate ring man and a superb boxer. Like so many others, Dixon
died broken in body, spirit, and wallet.

Pete Herman, bantam champ (1917–20), although a light
puncher (nineteen KO's in 148 fights), beat everyone in his division—and resoundingly. A. J. Liebling said he was the greatest
infighter he'd ever seen, and he'd seen plenty. In 1921, Herman,
nearly blind after nine years warring, fought Midgett Smith in
New York City by feint and touch. He would draw a punch and
as soon as he felt a glove or arm or a passing current of air, he
knew where Smith was. He lost the decision because he couldn't
see to follow up Smith at a distance. He could feint and fool you
with both hands out of sight. He could anticipate moves and lead
and counter and put his combination of punches together *at a*

John F. Gilbey

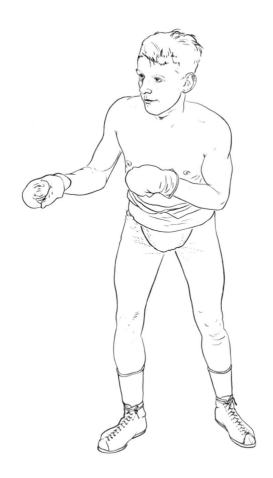

Jimmy Wilde

range of inches. Much of the smooth hand action that made the little Italian such an effective body puncher came from his early years spent shining shoes.

The Flyweights

Jim Wilde out of Wales deceived you. He had a spindly, emaciated appearance and a baby face. But his baby face weaned in boxing

Pancho Villa

booths (he may have fought four hundred bouts there) could do what few boxers ever could—hit perfectly straight with awesome power with both hands. He would suit his style to those who opposed him. In fact, he would fight a man using the man's own style just for kicks, and annihilate him. His forte though was the shadowy retreat, snapping and popping as he went, from which came the sobriquet, "The ghost with a hammer in each hand." In one hundred thirty-eight official glove matches he had a KO record of fifty-six percent and was defeated only four times and then only by men considerably heavier than he. The weight differential becomes more crucial the lighter the boxer. Wilde never weighed over a hundred pounds and thus gave a minimum of ten pounds away in each fight. When he was KO'd by Pete Herman in 1921 he gave Pete twenty-eight pounds!

Pancho Villa (Francisco Guilledo), a spectacular fighter from the Philippines, beat Wilde late in Jimmy's career (1923), but has

John F. Gilbey

to rank with him on the basis of his excellent record. He had a stinging jab and crossed brilliantly with his right. After losing a decision to the heavier Jimmy McLarnin in 1926, he developed blood poisoning from an ulcerated tooth and died. I don't know whether McLarnin did one of his celebrated somersaults at the end of the match. But after his death Jimmy, like the rest of the boxing fraternity, mourned the premature passing of this scrappy little man of boxing class.

Boxers truly were a fraternity. Sim Kessel in *Hanged at Auschwitz* tells how he, a former boxer, was standing outside the death-house at Auschwitz waiting his turn to be gassed when he noticed a Nazi guard with the battered look of an ex-pug. Kessel asked him about it and the guard affirmed it. They got to talking and found they had boxed in the same circuit and knew the same boxers. The upshot was that the guard loaded him on his motor-cycle and drove him back to the barracks.

Dirty Fighters

Class and fortitude they had . . . and also techniques that went beyond the rules. It was a tough racket. Bill Conn, interviewed after he had hit Bob Pastor in the groin three times, said, "You're not an altar boy in there." And Fritzie Zivic confided, "I'd give 'em the head, choke 'em, hit 'em in the balls, but I'd never gouge their eyes because I didn't want 'em to do that to me." He also said, "You're fighting, not playing a piano in there."

Many fighters fouled. "Elbows" McFadden liked to heel with the open glove. And Tony Galento ("I was a clean fighter; I always took a bath before the fight") would do anything he could get away with. Fritzie Zivic, called by W. C. Heinz "one of the all-time masters of the digital and cephalic phases of the Sweet Science," dreamed of owning a Cadillac. The day of his title fight with Henry Armstrong he went to peek at it. Later he recalled:

> "That night Henry's giving it to me pretty good and I can see that Cadillac rolling farther and farther away from me. Henry's giving me the elbows and the shoulders and the top of the head,

and I can give that stuff back pretty good, but I don't dare to or maybe they'll throw me out of the ring. Well in the seventh round I give him the head a couple times and choke him a couple times and use the elbow some, and the referee says: 'If you boys want to fight that way, it's okay with me.' 'Hot damn!' I told Luke Carney in my corner. 'Watch me go now.' And from there out I saw that Cadillac turn around and come rollin' back."

The story is plausible save for who started the stuff. Fritzie was never second in that department.

But even here class prevailed. For every dirty fighter, there were hundreds of clean ones. Take Ezzard Charles, for example. Charles who died in 1975 at fifty-three beat Jersey Joe Walcott twice but lost to him on a one-punch knockout in 1951. He was a surgeon in the ring; a consummate boxer. His big weakness—if that's what it was—is that he'd get you in trouble and then he wouldn't finish you. He had that fatal malady—he was a nice guy. He may have been influenced somewhat by having Sam Baroudi, a fighter he kayoed, die after the fight. After retiring and while being savaged by a muscle-debilitating disease, he summed himself up: "Just a simple, square sort of fellow, who believed in playing the game by the rules. But if I had it to do over again, I wouldn't change a thing."

Products of Hard Times

In fact, given their environment, it's surprising there weren't more dirty fighters. The soil they sprang from made for dirt-tough men. Only Corbett came out of a bank. There were few if any other white collar workers willing or able to take the stresses of the ring. Dempsey was a miner; Johnson, a longshoreman; Fitzsimmons and Les Darcy, smiths; McAuliffe, a cooper who pounded hoops on barrels; and Jeffries was a boilermaker in an era when rivets had to be pounded in by hand.

Rigorous life in a growing industrial nation made for extremely hard men. Ketchel learned to fight in a hobo jungle where survival was often tougher than in a real jungle. There fighting was no sportive endeavor but often a matter of life or death. You were nurtured on violence unredeemed by rules. And when Ketchel moved up to the ring only once did he forget the lessons of the old days. In a rematch with Billy Papke (whom he'd beaten) Ketchel made the mistake of extending his gloves at the outset in the time-honored ritual only to be suckered by Papke and finally done away with in the twelfth round (Ketchel of course returned the favor in the third fight).

Boxers were recruited from the lower socioeconomic levels. The rank order of the number of prominent boxers of various ethnic groups from 1909 to 1948 was as follows:

	1	2	3
1909	Irish	German	English
1916	Irish	German	Italian
1928	Jewish	Italian	Irish
1936	Italian	Irish	Jewish
1948	Negro	Italian	Mexican

Black Boxers

Blacks have continued their dominance to the present. Hemingway had a line on black boxers modified from Villon which went, "Où sont les nègres d'antan." (Where are the blacks of yesteryear?") He was obviously looking back from his Paris vantage in the 1920s to the period graced by Johnson, Jeannette, McVey, the Dixie Kid, Langford, and others who boxed in Europe when they couldn't find fights in America. In fact, the real father of boxing in France and Germany, according to Nat Fleischer, was Bobby Dobbs, a black who operated boxing schools in Paris and Berlin.

In our list of bests above, seven of the sixteen were black. And when he was asked, Jack Johnson said the best boxers of all time were Dixon, Gans, and Walcott. Add to these men like Jeannette, McVey, Jack Blackburn, Wills, Robinson, and Jeff Clark (the "Old Joplin Ghost") and you sing quite a melody.

Joe Jeannette was superb. It has been said that he lost a close duke to Johnson and "L'il Artha" would not meet him again. Not true: they fought nine times, Joe winning one on a foul, losing two decisions, not counting two draws and four no decisions.

Sam McVey was not only a fine stylist, he was also recorded as the ugliest man who ever entered the ring. But I have a bronze of him and I must say I've seen many worse specimens. (I grant that the boxing breed can't be characterized as handsome, the only comely ones I can think of were: Benny Leonard, George Carpentier, Jack Britton, Young Stribling, Ray Robinson, and Gene Tunney.) In 1909, in one of the classic Jeannette-McVey fights (they went to it five times), Jeannette was down twenty-one times in the first nineteen rounds. McVey didn't go down until the thirty-ninth but thereafter fell another eighteen times, Jeannette winning in the fiftieth.

Many forget that Jack Blackburn, who reared Joe Louis to the heavyweight championship, had an incomparable record as a lightweight. Twenty years after he started fighting he lost his first and last two fights by KO. But in the interim he fought Gans, O'Brien, Langford, and Greb to draws or in no decision fights. And they forget Jeff Clark who gave away weight always but still managed to beat luminaries like Wills and Langford.

There were others of course but these were the princes. I hear screams about my not including Henry Armstrong in this august company. But Armstrong, though he held three titles at once, and was a great presser and winger, had neither a good jab nor any follow-on authority in his right, so he has to trail the ones cited above.

Favorite Tactics

Jim Jeffries' best punch was a left hook to the body out of a low crouch. Joe Louis, beside being a reflexive counterer, had a fine left jab, not as fast as Tunney's, but much more punishing. Jack Johnson's uppercut was probably the best in history and he was the only boxer able to use it retreating. Kid Gavilan used a bolo punch straight out of the Cuban sugar-cane fields. Kid McCoy was famous for his corkscrew left to the body executed by twisting the wrist. Carpentier had a one-two left jab/right cross as fast and lethal as that of anyone ever serving up this orthodox sequence.

The best jabs of the recent era (since 1925) belonged to Leonard, Louis, Tunney, Sharkey, and Braddock. Leonard, Louis, and Tunney coupled theirs with all-round ability. Sharkey was inconsistent and Braddock had nothing except fortitude.

Probably the hardest right hand puncher of recent memory was Aurelio Herrera who recorded a KO ratio of nearly sixty percent across eighty-one and beat good lightweights such as Young Corbett (1906). The Maxes, Baer and Schmeling, also had powerful right hands. Max Baer's was good but not good enough to compensate for a weak left and strong clowning. With that mix he couldn't survive. And didn't. In his match with Braddock, the slow Irisher simply circled leftward away from the right, and Baer didn't have enough left hand to stop the tactic.

Both Dempsey and Jeffries fought from a crouch, but with a difference, Jeffries was big and would bull in and bury his left hook in an opponent's body to bring the curtains together. But Dempsey was a wolverine who had trained in a four-foot high cage with the result he could do anything offensively and defensively from the crouch. And when he exploded out of it, as Willard found out, it was like a beast emerging who never intended to be caged again. The animal roles were reversed ludicrously in his match with Firpo "The Bull of the Pampas" who claimed to have knocked out an ox but who ran *on all fours* with Dempsey pursuing him like a gaucho in their legendary bout.

Some claim that Dempsey's hands were loaded with plaster of paris when he demolished Willard. I doubt it. For one thing, adding any weight to your fists meant they were heavier to hold up and thus would ultimately work to your disadvantage. But this drawback didn't keep many lower-class boxers from such trickery. Some used the knots of their laces to rub against their opponent's face in a clinch. (Later of course rules required taping of the knots.) And you could use more gauze and tape than were legally permitted if you were willing to suffer the penalty the added weight exacted—slower hands, particularly on defense. Joe Jacobs, Schmeling's manager, wouldn't let Louis have his usual twelve feet of gauze and six feet of tape, and Louis, in the first fight, sprained both thumbs as a result and lost the fight.

Corbett invented shadow boxing. He could feint with his eyebrows. Later in life he praised William "Young" Stribling as being the best feinter of the current crop. It's true, Stribling could feint you out of your socks. Where a Corbett or a Young Griffo would feint you silly they often would not or could not follow up on the feint. But Stribling could. He would feint with his left hand, then his right, then after a moment's hesitation he'd bomb you with his right—his famed buckshot punch.

One of the few modern boxers able to punch inside of hooks instead of just blocking them, Stribling is well worth a brief digression. He had an exceptional record but fought far too often and was burned out and exploited by his family. He ended up hating the sport and would do or talk about anything as long as the subject was not boxing. He played pro basketball for a time, flew an airplane, and golfed. He ended by killing himself on a motorcycle.

His KO record was a whooping forty-nine percent. Despite this he missed success because, like Ezzard Charles, he disliked hurting a man. So he'd get a man in trouble and then let him recover. He hated training and almost never did it; he felt the nearly three hundred fights he engaged in served just as well. If he had been managed by someone other than his father and had fought no more than half the fights he did, and if he'd trained properly in compensation, he would have been heavyweight champion even without the killer instinct. Sharkey and Schmeling, who both beat him, would not have been able to stay with him, Schmeling because he had no left jab, and Sharkey—who had an excellent left jab—because he was too inconsistent.

Another great feinter was Abe Attell, former feather champ. A guy who had some unsavory connections, Attell lost only ten of one hundred seventy bouts, "some unintentionally" as Red Smith wrote. He was another example of excellence who might have been the best ever if he could have concentrated on his craft instead of, in his case, on horses and gambling.

John F. Gilbey

Keep Cool, Fool

Three of the coolest under fire were Tunney, Tommy Loughran, and Carpentier—this assessment based on their general demeanor. But there were others quite as cool. Little Jimmy Wilde was too impassive even to look bored while Pal Moore strutted and stamped "like an ancient Chinese warrior" just before a match in which Jimmy boxed his ears off (1919).

The amazing young Griffo always looked drunk. Looked—hell, he usually was drunk. The Dixie Kid was a master of appearing to be out on his feet, drawing an avid customer in, and then belting him out.

Coolness is composure under stress and none developed it better than Battling Nelson. This cyclone was usually too busy to be blase' but when the ambience darkened he would never give up. Christy Williams put him down forty-two times before Nelson turned the tables and KO'd him in the seventeenth round. No wonder he was called "The Durable Dane."

Can a Little Man Beat a Big One?

The portrait author Jim Tully paints of Jerry Wayne,* a fighter in an insane asylum, is sad, but just as sad is the true story of Primo Carnera, a big lug ("The Ambling Alp" they called him) who couldn't fight a little. Imported from Italy, this giant won a gang of pretend matches promoted by gangland and then got demolished when the tanking stopped. Although Carnera had beaten Jack Sharkey in a smeller, he was never accused of being a fighter. Carnera couldn't knock your hat off but he was the proximate occasion of death for Ernie Shaaf. Carnera hit poor Ernie with a left jab that wouldn't have broken an egg and Ernie collapsed, to die a few days later. Ernie actually was killed six months earlier

---

*In *The Bruiser* (1936).

in a match in which he was annihilated by Max Baer, a man who could hit.

Later Carnera turned to wrestling and further ridicule. In Europe he had begun as a wrestler but was lousy even at that trade. Yukio Tani, the small judo "Pocket Hercules," once let Carnera get a standing lock on him in London, shifted his weight, extricated, turned Carnera on his ear, and then said: "See, no balance." At the end Carnera dying of cirrhosis was likened by Red Smith to "a whale on a flatcar." A poor gentle freak manipulated and broken, he was just another casualty of boxing.

Am I saying that a good little man will beat a good big man: Nope. A good rule of thumb is: bet the weight. However, a good little boxer will usually box the ears off a big country boy who has never had gloves on. But not always, even against unpolished hicks. Ralph Ellison in his classic *Invisible Man* (1952) wrote:

> Once I saw a prize fighter boxing a yokel. The boxer was swift and amazingly scientific. His body was one violent flow of rapid rhythmic action. He hit the yokel a hundred times while the yokel held up his arms in stunned surprise. But suddenly the yokel, rolling about in a gale of boxing gloves, struck one blow and knocked science, speed, and footwork as cold as a well-digger's posterior. The smart money hit the canvas . . . The yokel had simply stepped inside of his opponent's sense of time.

Does Age Wither?

I saw Jack Johnson and Jess Willard in a 25¢ sideshow in Los Angeles in 1944. They didn't square off: the quarter was just to see them and hear them talk a little. Both were big, but only Johnson looked like he could still go three slam-bang minutes. In fact, the next year Jack (age 65) did box an exhibition with Joe Jeannette (age 66).

But this was honorific fighting. On the real side, Joe Walcott won the heavy championship at 37; Bob Fitzsimmons the light-heavy at 41 (he was just getting started at 30 and knocked out Corbett at 35); and Ray Robinson the middle at 37. And ageless

John F. Gilbey

Archie Moore was still lightheavy king at 43.

But generally age does wither as often as custom stales. In 1931 the 36-year old Dempsey wanted to challenge Schmeling for the title. To prove himself he boxed forty-two opponents in thirteen cities in thirty days. But none of it mattered. The reason: none of them were the calibre of the German. Quality counts. Invariably boxers trying to come back find that time and chance happeneth to all, that the reflexes need be just a bit off for old man disaster to barge in.

Gentle Boxers and Uncaring Managers

Some years back writing in a karate magazine, a physiologist tried to establish that boxers are crueller than other people. R. W. Smith demolished him in argument by attacking his logic without necessarily siding with boxers. Let me do that now. Boxers *outside the ring* are the gentlest of men. Seldom have I met a bad egg. Other sports turn out guys meaner than junkyard dogs with far greater regularity than boxing.

In fact, boxers are too gentle and trusting. Carnera once made $700,000 in six months and didn't see a penny of it. Johnny Saxton made a quarter million and ended up broke, jugged for burglary, and finally committed as mentally incompetent. Randy Turpin, who beat Sugar Ray, ended up working in a junkyard, and later shot himself. And poor old Beau Jack, after holding a championship and making a million dollars ended back at the same shoeshine stand in Miami from which he started. These are but a few examples: the list of poor gullible guys taken to the financial cleaners by crooked or uncaring managers is endless.

Suffice to say there were few who really cared about their charges. Most wanted the money and prestige attached to the fighter, but that was about it. Willie Pep once put it: "I had the bravest manager in the world—he didn't care who I fought." Ditto for many trainers: Tunney after being drubbed silly by Greb was told by his trainer the next day: "You really caused me a lot of work last night, kid, closing all those cuts." Fighters found much solace in the words of their handlers as they were pushed out to the attack: "Go on kid, he can't hurt *us!*"

But Wilson Mizner cared. This wit managed Ketchel for a time. Coming into Ketchel's hotel room the afternoon of a big fight he found Stan smoking marijuana in bed with two blondes. Asked later what he did, Mizner said: "What could I do? I told them to move over!"

Joking aside, Jack Hurley was an exception. He was an honest manager and an exceptionally good one. Writer Paul Gallico said he was the only manager he'd ever seen who had any feeling for his fighters. He loved them and they all broke his heart. He could do everything. He was great in the corner and at closing cuts with Monsel's Solution, one drop of which can cause blindness. And at training a man in the way he should go: Vince Foster boxed too wide, thus sacrificing speed for wallop and getting hit too much in the process. So Hurley joined his feet with a strip of innertube and that did the trick.

The best fighter Jack ever had was Billy Petrolle, "The Fargo Express," who boxed from 1922 to 1934, meeting six world champs and beating men the calibre of Canzoneri, McLarnin, and Battalino. Petrolle had a KO record of forty percent and was so tough he actually beat Jimmy McLarnin who had one of the biggest punches of anyone in the 1930s (pound-for-pound, of course), and he won by punching not boxing (Jimmy outboxed him in two later goes).

Jack Blackburn, an excellent fighter in his prime, was the trainer who guided Joe Louis to the boxing heights. Jack couldn't get across to the dazed Louis how Schmeling was getting his deadly right in during their first fight in 1936 because Joe just couldn't learn and change his style *during a fight*, but you can be sure Jack was trying.

Toward the last, Jack had arthritis bad and had trouble getting up the steps to the apron. This touched Joe and he told Jack that he'd only have to come up once in the second Buddy Baer fight (1943). He did: Joe knocked Buddy out in the first stanza.

John F. Gilbey

The Current Crop

I do not rank any heavy since Marciano as top quality. Liston and Foreman were musclebound; Frazier and Holmes had only one hand; and Ali was the most overrated fighter in history. Joe Louis once told Ali that he ought to go to jail even for dreaming that he could beat the Bomber. Red Smith wrote how Ali once asked Louis: "Joe, you really think you coulda whup me?" "When I was champion," Joe said, "I went on what they called a bum-of-the-month tour." Ali snarled: "You saying I'm a bum?' Joe looked him square in the eyes and said: "You woulda been on the tour."

Two data are all that are necessary to demolish Ali as a fighter. (As a guy I like his humor* and I bow to him for his lonely stand against the Vietnam lunacy). One, he gave his opponents free shots at his middle. Two, he lay back on the ropes—the rope-a-dope—as a tactic in order to tire his opponent. Ali could not have done either of these things against *any* ranking heavy in the thirties. He would have been taken out instantly. You could make a mistake then and with luck get by with it. But you couldn't make the same mistake continually.

George Foreman not long ago delayed a $35 million fight because of a cut over his eye. Tony Galento commented on this in his usual raucous way, saying that next fighters would wear lace on their pants. Tony said that once he had his chin cut open by a beer mug and in forty-eight hours he was in the ring with Max Baer. And the little gamecock, Tommy Farr, cut his eye five

---

*Western boxing doesn't have the tradition of nonsense surrounding the Asian variety, but it's had its share of dillies. Lou Nova was going to beat Louis with a "cosmic" punch derived from yoga, remember? He didn't. And Archie Moore used a secret breathing, inhaling through his ears, which was supposed to prevent his getting tired. Needless to say, he got tired. And Ali had plenty of esoterica. These things are pleasant press-agentries, hypes not meant to be taken seriously.

days before his bout with Braddock and refused to welch on the fight (incidentally, Farr was a durable cuss, his first fight being in 1926 and his last in 1953). They were a different breed.

Gene Tunney rightly called Floyd Patterson the "absolute novice." Patterson boxed peek-a-boo with his feet on a line, a posture conducive to being knocked down. Patterson was. And often.

And so on. You get the idea. The other weights? I don't know, I see them so seldom anymore. Bob Foster was a happy exception. He moved well and was a vicious puncher for a lightheavy and could have survived in the 1930s. Some recent fighters who could have boxed fifty years ago were Ray Leonard, Roberto Duran, Tommy Hearns, and Wilfredo Gomez. But today's boxers for the most part use their legs for dancing and posturing rather than punching. Most current champions are arm punchers who learn more from celluloid fantasies like the egregious 5'9" Sylvester Stallone's "Rocky" series than from real gym workouts.

No one is to blame for the drastic drop in quality since the 1930s. You can't have quality unless you have the pool to draw on. Competition thrives on numbers. In 1938 there were eight thousand professional boxers in America, one thousand eight hundred of them black. And at least treble that number in amateur boxing. Every town of thirty thousand had weekly matches for which the amateurs got a buck a round for starters. There were clubs everywhere. In those depression years we lived close to struggle and pain,* and this, not affluence and the hype, is the compound out of which good boxing must come.

The old pugilists put in seven hours a day, much of it in roadwork. Corbett at thirty-four boxed twenty rounds a day in preparation for Jeffries. In the 1930s—still a good decade—if a fighter

---

*Physical pain is strange. It is intensely felt by only the one experiencing it. When it is over, an unusual happiness ensues. But once ended, try as you might, you can't remember it. This is nature's way of letting us survive: if we could remember vividly all our past pains it would shatter our psyches.

John F. Gilbey

trained two hours daily he was considered a workhorse. Nowadays boxers train rarely if at all. They spend their time in night club singing acts, on talk shows, at casinos, and the like. Tony Zale said that a body punch he used on Al Hostak took ten years in the gym to perfect. Today there are few gyms and no gym fighters. That is why there are no boxers left. No one wants to train and sweat for ten years to develop a body punch which may not even be the decisive blow in a given fight.

Rocky Marciano was the last good gym fighter. He was a beaut and ate up the sweat-heavy dulldom of training. But I don't rank him with the very best, simply because he was a lunger and didn't know a whole lot about boxing. Rocky had the shortest arms of modern heavy, and lacking the boxing skills, had to lunge to get in close with his dynamite.

Babe Ruth observed once: "I swing as hard as I can and I try to swing right through the ball. In boxing, your fist usually stops when you hit a man, but it's possible to hit so hard that your fist doesn't stop. I try to follow through the same way."

That was Rocky's metier. He would surge in, both stubby arms swinging and pumping and he'd get every last ounce of power into his fists. This worked in a lackluster period, but it wouldn't have worked against Sharkey's left jab or Schmeling's right cross. Still he was the last of the good heavyweights.

Nearing the close of this chapter on a sport that is deservedly dying, I quote the late gifted sportswriter Don Skene: "Things were never like this when we fought on barges."

Great Boxing Reporters

The first and best boxing reporter/historian was Pierce Egan (1772–1849) an autodidact who flourished in the first three decades of the nineteenth century. His *Boxiana*, which was published in five separate volumes between 1812 and 1829, was both a history and a weekly account of pugilism. Egan made fighters come alive. He believed the sport had style and he added imagination to it, even giving it its own unique vocabulary. His language had a resonance all its own. "The Frenchman very soon got milled and, shortly afterward, mizzled . . . " Egan created a literary genre, and when prizefighting waned he was finished—or, in his words, "blowed up, nobbered, dished, queered, cut up and tipped."

The last great boxing reporter and a man who knew boxing intimately was the late Nat Fleischer. His writing was without grace, his output staggering, but his insights good. Fleischer did much first-rate research, but it was marred by his continual recourse to bromides. He would have been well advised to heed the admonition: avoid clichés like the plague.

Nor was Nat above romanticizing. In his book on Benny Leonard he wrote of a fight Leonard had with a Chinese named Ah Chung. The warring Hip Sing and Oh Leong tongs (gangs) filled the house to watch it. Leonard took Ah Chung out in the sixth and, sensing that the natives were restless, he ran for his dressing room. The tongs went at each other then in the street and a total of nine were carted off to the morgue. A great story but hardly credible. Especially when we know that Ah Chung was managed by the boy bandit Jimmy Johnston, and had a real name: Mickey Mulligan, which of course made him Irish, not Chinese."*

And Nat could be simply silly. The teens of this century happily saw the demise of the battle royal in which ten blacks were put into a ring and fought it out until only one man was left standing. About this reprehensible institution Nat Fleischer wrote:

> It was wholesale murder while it lasted. The victor was a gory sight to behold. But—what a hit it made with the crowd! We're more refined as regards our boxing shows nowadays (1938), but I sometimes think we miss a whole lot of fun that oldtimers had.

Nat should have tried it just once and it would have changed his idea of fun.

Not only are there no fighters anymore, there aren't even

---

*A real story in this genre occurred the day Johnson liquidated Jeffries in Reno in 1910. The toughest guy wasn't in the ring that day. The Hip Sing tong's number one executioner, Won Let, with thirty notches in his hatchet, was at ringside watching the fight.

John F. Gilbey

people left who recognize good fighting. Certainly there are no sportswriters like Red Smith. And no novelists or short story writers comparable to Hemingway, Nelson Algren, and W. Heinz. So this has left the field to novelists like Norman Mailer and Wilfrid Sheed and high-toned journalists like Garry Wills doing their in-depth reportage and making big bucks. None of them knows anything about boxing. And none are Hazlitts.* The silly Mailer once likened a good lay to a fast fifteen-round fight. How would he know?

Mailer has also written that boxing is the most intellectual of all sports. Utter nonsense. Almost any sport is superior to it in the area of the intellect. Boxing is a one-on-one proposition in which power, distance, and timing are crucial. An appreciation of these factors comes from feel, from experience, and from proper training, none of which has much to do with intellect. In fact, you could argue compellingly that intellect stands in the way of a fighter. It protests the pain he must suffer and dish out. He must accommodate that pain or enter another pursuit.

Nope, you don't look for intelligence in boxers any more than in novelists. Wilson Mizner, the greatest wit America ever produced, said that Tom Sharkey was so dumb that for two years he went out of the saloon he bought by crawling under the doors—he never realized they swung both ways.

And so in this age of media hype you have know-nothings paying to watch do-nothings. Non-boxers like Ali and Holmes make seven million smackers for ineffectually mauling each other and millions of fans are satisfied they've seen a fight. All this, sayeth the Buddha, is illusion.

The Ethics of Boxing

A friend told me once that if sportswriters knew elementary anat-

---

* William Hazlitt's account of a fight between William Neat and Thomas Hickman (Dec. 11, 1821) remains the best description of a pugilistic contest.

omy they would never shill for boxing. I rejoined that what they needed more than elementary anatomy was elementary ethics.

For, despite my years of participating in and watching it, I must conclude that boxing is bad. Bad for the boxer and for the audience. Why? Because it is the only sport that has injury of the opponent as its aim. This sterile intentionality makes the sport a destructive thing—whereas life should be creative. Even the manic football so popular now in America does not posit injury as its goal (though injury is part and parcel of the points which are its goal). A footballer faces the risk of pain; a boxer, the certainty of it. Boxing guarantees that you will be hurt. Sure, there were consummate boxers like Benny Leonard who never needed to comb his hair, but they all got hurt at some time or other.

Paul Gallico, an excellent journalist (who was foolhardy enough to try conclusions with Dempsey once) wisely saw boxing for what it was. Gallico originated the Golden Gloves tournaments, but later concluded that boxing ought to be banned. It brought out, he wrote, the worst in the boxers and the spectators. It had no value as physical culture and was lamentable as self-defense. He believed that the fist, composed of tiny, fragile articulated bones and cartilages set on the wrist, is an ineffective weapon.

On ethical grounds I agree with his view, but not on functional. Granted the fist is fragile, but instrumented properly and manipulated efficiently, it is a power in the street. Even with the qualitative slough into which boxing has sunk, the average boxer will still take your champion *karateka* nine times out of ten.

I know that a wrestler will usually prevail over a boxer and I've seen too many street fights cancel out boxers in the street (Mickey Walker* reportedly was once bested by a 140-pound busboy in New York City), but give them their due: boxers can handle themselves against most mortals on the pavement.

Gallico was right about spectators. I have seen hundreds of

---

*Walker lost his middle crown in 1925 to Harry Greb. That night after the fight the pair of them did a repeat in the street but history doesn't relate who won that one.

John F. Gilbey

fights and the bellicosity of the fans always scares me. A head blow that can cause brain damage and even kill a man, they applaud. But a punch to the groin which will hurt a man but seldom knock him out, they boo. The explanation I'm afraid, is Freudian. Similarly, in Violenceville (American TV) everything is okayed except kicks to the groin. Nope, the boxing crowd's expectant "He's hurt" reminds a reincarnated gladiator like me of the "Habet" ("He's wounded") when I was speared once in Rome.

The British journal *Psychological Medicine* years ago showed that the brains of fifteen boxers, including two of former world champions, had damage that could lead to insanity. And Dr. Nicholas Corsellis who headed a team at Runwell Hospital in Essex, England, researching the brains of boxers who fought between 1900–1940 found that most of the damage occurred to the most successful boxers. Why? Because they boxed more often. Add to this the fact that in any boxing population prior to 1950 over sixty percent were at least mildly punchdrunk.

Part of the problem is that our skulls aren't what they used to be. Scientists have found that 50,000 years ago we had massive skulls with few fracture lines. We no longer grow that bony protection. What we have evolved are skulls meant for something other than resisting repeated five hundred-pound blows.

Look at the brain. It is a three-pound mess of porridge suspended in fluid. Blows can cause it to bang against the sharp bony sphenoidal ridge it rests on, tearing the membrane and destroying tissues and cells. And brain cells once destroyed are dead forever—they can't be reconstituted. Wrapped in yards of gauze and encased in an eight-ounce glove the fist assumes some of the weight and rigidity of a hammer. A lightweight can deliver a punch with the impact of over five hundred pounds of pressure. Add this to the speed and direction of the opponent as he receives the blow and you have the potential for grievous brain damage.

Abe Simon, the old heavyweight, was something of a freak in that he never felt the punches served up to him by Joe Louis and other belters of the period. It may be that some organic aberration put his pain threshhold higher than most men's, but it doesn't mean he was without pain. Simon himself said that he had pain in his head constantly until he retired.

I've read that ten percent of pro boxers in the 1930s had retinal detachments (the retina is flimsier than tissue paper). It is bad enough for the eye to have to take punches from every conceivable angle but, worse, it must absorb butts, thumbs, and an occasional elbow as well. Add to that the Harry Grebses who love to heel it with the laces and gouges it until it is closed. Speaking of Harry, it is ironic that he fought with one bad eye for years, and died (1932) as a result of an operation on it. Canada Lee (Lionel Canagata) was a pretty good boxer (he fought three champions) until a detached retina pushed him into acting (if you never saw him as Bigger Thomas in *Native Son* or Stephen Kumalo in *Cry, Beloved Country*, you missed some fine performances). Double vision is also very common; one old battler expressed his woes well: "Yeah, I see two men in there; I hit the one that ain't there, and get bashed by the one who is there."

Besides ophthalmic injuries, maxillofacial and aural damage are also common. Not to mention damage further down. *The Journal of Urology* (1954) concluded that acute kidney trauma occurs in sixty-five to eighty-nine percent of boxers during a fight and is manifested by post-bout hematuria. Body blows are only less injurious than shots to the head. They *still* damage. For this reason Dr. A. Steinhaus' proposal that an additional foul zone—above the shoulders—be established would still not meet my objections. Although the proposal would certainly reduce the incidence of subdural hemorrhage which caused fifteen of twenty-one boxers killed in New York City in 1918–50 to shuffle off this mortal coil, it would still leave the vulnerable body as a target. And it would ruin the sport as a promotion: it would not satisfy the fans' lust for blood.

So what is the alternative? Is there a solution? Sure—ban it! Iceland has prohibited the sport, and it is severely circumscribed in Belgium and Scandanavia. Plus, the father of the bloody business, England, is now moving to ban it. The Catholic Church is against boxing but is, as usual, silent. The church that Camus blasted for not excoriating Hitler, says that boxing is essentially an American problem and that the American Bishops should act

John F. Gilbey

on it. This is the same rationalizing cop-out that Rome used on the Vietnam problem, but did the American Bishops respond on that mess? They did not.

The point has been well made that the change from London Prize Ring rules actually made the sport more brutal. Thereafter, gloves protected fists and permitted boxers to fight many more bouts in a career. No longer could a fighter take a fall if he were in trouble and thus get thirty-eight seconds of rest; now he had to stand until the three-minute round was over. Stand and suffer. This is not to say that pugilism was not brutal—it was—but only to say that the Queensberry rules didn't dilute it much, if at all.

Some have argued that a return to bareknuckles might reduce injuries. It's a good point. The ungloved fist, regardless of how it's toughened (by pickling it in brine and so on) is a pretty fragile object. Standup fighting, bareknuckled, with wrestling and infighting barred, would reduce injuries. But it would still not meet my basic objection to boxing—namely, the ethical one. Boxing would still be uncivilized, still the sadistic brutal thing that Bertrand Russell called it in 1922.

Like bull-baiting and other blood activities, boxing is a pseudomasculine "sport" that should have no place in civilized society. Its continuation only means that our psyches are sick as hell. The rise of women in the West and the concomitant levelling of the masses could be a healthy thing. But, so far, the vanguard of the women's movement, instead of diluting macho, is compounding the problem by injecting even more aggression and violence into it. Over time it is hoped that the *yin* that is their nature will castrate (forgive an ugly word but it seems the only right one here) the pseudomasculinity of the harsher segment of what passes for civilization in the so-called "developed" nations nowadays.

Boxing also produces madness and suicides. Offhand, I can think of such greats as Joe Grim, Mike McTigue, Ad Wolgast, and Battling Nelson—all committed to insane asylums. Ironically, the last two met in 1910 in a slugfest which Wolgast won in the fortieth. Poor Wolgast is best remembered for that but also for the near double KO in his encounter with Joe Rivers, an excellent

Mexican fighter, in 1912. Wolgast hit him a clean shot and Rivers, falling, kneed him (accidentally?) in the groin. Both went down. The confused referee sure as hell wasn't going to count two men out and so helped Wolgast to his feet and declared him the winner. So the fans will remember the "Michigan Wildcat" and his victories over Nelson and Rivers. But not the nuthouse part—that they don't want to think about.

Joe Grim, who fought early in the century, is known today (if at all) not for the fact that he went bananas, but that he was boxing's most durable man. Experts say he was never knocked out in 250 bouts. Actually he was KO'd three times (Burke, McVey, and Zeringer).

And suicides: Billy Papke, Kid McCoy, and Randy Turpin are three I can readily remember. The last two made considerable money—McCoy over a million dollars in the movies. But as one writer said about Turpin: "After poor investments, women, and spongers had taken his money, all that was left was a gun in the attic."

Sure there is heroism, sacrifice, discipline, and courage in boxing—and in abundance. But at base it is a cruel bloody sport and, like dog, cock, and bull fighting, ought to be outlawed. I respect deeply many of the men and the high skills with which they graced the ring, but the injuries, deaths, suicides, and broken hearts are not worth the candle. The shining qualities referred to above can be gotten through sports (wrestling and judo,* for example) that are sensibly limited and thus creative. If karate kept to the code it had in Asia, it might function as a good substitute for boxing. With limited contact and stress put on skillful attack and defense it would be a useful surrogate indeed. Restraint is

---

*Al Holtmann of the San Diego Judo Club hoped that judo could replace boxing. It's a thought. Judo is variable and efficient and can be a crowd pleaser. But so far it had failed to find an audience. The players in the U.S. outnumber the watchers. Politics have riddled the judo movement, egos have crushed Kano's rationale for humility, and ignorance generally rules.

John F. Gilbey

the key here as in all of life.

The commercial demands are such, however, that violence must out. The crowd still wants Barabbas: they require blood and knockouts. Go to a match and watch them, not the boxers. The mob will momentarily sympathize with poor Johnny Owen, killed before TV cameras in 1980 and Duk-koo Kim in 1982, and then they'll be back in their chairs the next week howling. A dose of such a debased humanity should be an antidote to any fan's craving for the fight.

In the closing paragraph of V. Blasco-Ibanez's *Blood and Sand* (1908) the gored matador is doing his last "faena" on a cot while another "fight" is in progress. The crowd roars. The book ends: "Outside roared the beast, the real beast, the only beast!"

WORLD WRESTLING

"There ain't a holt that can't be broke."
— Tom Jenkins, American champion (1897–1906)

I hitchhiked into Omaha in August 1936, arriving with nineteen cents in my pocket. I got on at a warehouse after three days of stretching those coins. But that was in the days when you could get a plate lunch—meat, spuds, and vegetable—coffee, and a cross-barred slab of gooseberry pie in left field, all for a quarter. And in that Depression time that was exactly what I got for one hour of picking up ninety-pound crates of canned turkey and other sundries. Now hefting hundred-pound bags of potatoes or 120-pound stalks of bananas poses no problem—you simply toss them over your shoulder. But a compact wood carton weighing ninety pounds has to be picked up and handled chiefly by the arms. Unloading hundreds of these a day makes babies of strong men.

But I was young then and revelled in the exertion. So much so that after a gruelling day I'd go down to one of the wrestling gyms in this, the best wrestling town in America, and put in a couple hours sweating with the local boys.

Early this century hundreds of wrestling gyms were set up in the backs of poolhalls and taverns in Omaha making the city the wrestling mecca of America. No wrestler of any worth ever bypassed the place. This was where the real thing happened, where you won your spurs or took up another trade.

In Omaha I learned wrestling and its peculiar patois. Begin with "show" and "shoot." To show means to wrestle for money, that is to play-act and cooperate with an opponent in order to deceive the public and loosen it from its moolah. For it is easier to polish and garnish the thing into high dives, acrobatic throws, and gimmicked techniques that will bilk the uninitiated than it is to "shoot"—that is, to wrestle competitively. Showing lets you "wrestle" every night with your opponent, while the promoters stage match patterns and championships that will produce big bucks. Showing is a burlesque, a caricature of real wrestling, and demeans the men doing it. It is dishonest and ought to be banned. It persists only because it produces enough revenue to buy ads in newspapers, resulting subsequently in free publicity and false legitimacy. When someone who prizes real wrestling squawks, the press responds that of course it's fake but as long as it's popular it's news and should be printed (by which, of course, the publisher means that as long as it produces revenue for the media, the media will go along with the lie).

The fraudulent play-acting that passes for wrestling now in America bears little resemblance to one of the world's oldest and most honorable sports. The only legitimate forms of wrestling still practiced here are high school, college, AAU-sponsored free-style, Graeco-Roman, and judo meets. If a man is a shooter he will not be in the pro circuit. He may still be wrestling in dirty YMCA's, but he will not make any money and he will often have trouble even finding a training partner.

It's too bloody bad. Wrestling was once popular here, and is still the national sport of countries as diverse as Japan, India, Pakistan, Turkey, Switzerland, Iceland, Great Britain, and the USSR. Besides the lust for money, global technology is the other culprit dragging real wrestling down. Traditionally a rural regional sport, wrestling has lost integrity as the bright lights and video stage come rolling in. Show wrestling unfortunately is not limited to America. Sped by ethicless commercialism, burlesque has crept into wrestling almost everywhere. So the expressions "show" and "shoot" now transcend national boundaries. The most telling example of this are the near sacred sumo and judo in which one sees team- and stable-mates diving for each other.

Plus, the nihilism of the times contributes. The need for a winner means you cut corners, shade the rules, fix the match. This cry for a winner has always struck me as a whimper of youngsters who never grew up.* After all, Odysseus and Ajax fought it out sinew against sinew until the referee, Achilles, called it a draw. And neither lost an iota of value, no diminution, by not being adjudged a winner. Baron de Coubertin and Grantland Rice were right—winning is in participating honestly—but try telling that to the newspapers!

It is curious that only carnivores (meat-eating) species wrestle, and only the short-jawed ones at that. There are exceptions to this of course (bears, snakes) but the rule holds up pretty well.

One expert has said that both dancing and procreation derive from wrestling. I grant wrestling the first, but not the last. The guy was in a library too long, I fear. If he'd ever been in a bedroom he'd know that procreation is instinctual—and has equipment irrelevant to wrestling.

It brings up an interesting question however, which bears on the philosophical: Is boxing older than wrestling? We know that sex is older than either. And it is fair to speculate that wrestling derived from the sex act—first as a playful, amorous frolic. Later the same sex found it permitted a controlled method of sportive activity. Almost certainly boxing had no such antecedent. It evolved from fighting to the death to become a more or less refined method of testing strength and stamina.

Thus wrestling can be said to be creative and loving in genesis, whereas boxing has derived from the destructive. Wrestling is older and, based on the embrace, is closer to love. Boxing, on the other hand, collides and pushes out, and ends by estranging. That's why I call wrestling honorable and why I lament the crookery now infecting much of it.

Back to Omaha. I loved the town and stayed a while, learn-

---

*Vince Lombardi, whose name is sacred to American football fans, was a ridiculous symbol of this nonsense. I like to remember Vince as a poor college student, a tough lineman at Fordham and later college coach struggling along with his wife eating hash. Not the later little martinet who refused to let his wife eat pie in training camp because the players weren't allowed to have it.

ing wrestling much as a craftsman used to learn now-dead arts such as manuscript illumination or fine stone-carving. With hours and labor and attention to detail.

I was lucky. I had many fine teachers and wrestled with or watched such greats as Jack Sherry, Karl Pojello, and other fine shooters. All they asked of you was that you showed up prepared to wrestle. And that you could live with pain. (E. J. Harrison, an excellent British *judoka* at the turn of the century,* and Jim Bregman, the American Judo Olympic medalist in the 1960s, went through much the same ordeal in Tokyo).

After Omaha my life took on its own direction. Wherever I went, I'd wrestle. Mostly for the fun and skill of it. But I would make some jingle occasionally from it when a carnival coincided with my stay in a place.

The old carnies usually were part of a flesh show. In between the contortionists and the strip-artists out on the platform would come the house grappler as ugly as sin and muscular as hell. His shill or mouthpiece would announce that this wonder would take on anyone in the crowd for five smackers. Most of the time the house had a plant out front who would accept the challenge. He'd look the part of a yokel and was always a bit bigger than the challenger—this to stimulate interest. Just like pro wrestling today, owning both grapplers let the house control the proceedings. It didn't matter who won—both guys were on salary. And both had techniques as bad as their breath. But this wouldn't work for too long in the same place. So then they'd have to accept legit wrestlers from the crowd. Even then if the guy looked good they'd try to make an arrangement.

I'd con the con-artists. I would stand up close and holler and stumble awkwardly toward the platform. I was young, skinny, baby-faced, and hung my head a lot in those days and this would help the deception. They would invariably accept me—once. Because when we got inside and the crowd had paid its dollar or

---

*His *The Fighting Spirit of Japan* (1913), a classic on the martial arts, was reprinted in the U.S. in 1982.

John F. Gilbey

so I'd pin the house man without ceremony. The house guy usually wasn't good enough to be dirty. But he'd try. He would elbow and jab me in close with his palm, try to strangle me, and pretend to throw me while getting into my gonads with an errant "accidental" foot. But regardless how strong a man is, none of this will work unless he has a measure of skill. And most of them didn't.

A couple of times I had my hands full. Sometimes a good wrestler down on his luck or simply as a diversion from the day's work at the papermill would do a short carny stint. Such wrestlers weren't content simply to pin you once you'd given them some trouble. They then hooked and ripped. In wrestling parlance, a hooker is a guy who works you into a leverage position where he forces you to submit through a hammerlock, wristlock, or toehold. He simply hooks one of your limbs until you shout uncle. A pinner pins you; a hooker makes you quit. And the hooking is not done according to the text: it is done forcefully and no quarter given until you yell. From this position, he'd stretch you a bit.

That is bad enough. It is still wrestling and you can quit anytime. But the ripper was a guy who would break your arm or leg and then ask afterward if you've had enough. He doesn't hear you surrender until his savagery is spent. He will get his hold maliciously over-leveraged and not stop until something snaps. He doesn't ask you to quit until you're on a stretcher.

Gotch was a hooker, a wild man in the ring, but when he got his toehold on you he'd let you crawl off bloody and bowed. Jack Sherry, on the other hand, was an out-and-out ripper who only left you when you were bloody and broken. For this reason he was feared and avoided by the pros. But that's only part of the reason. No one wrestled Jack because he seldom played; he was strictly a shooter and would not take orders from the combines that control wrestling.

Anyhow, I beat a good hooker once, but it took some time. He had age and experience and thirty pounds on me. So I got behind him and rode him for a half hour and he finally got so frustrated I was able to scissor him and maneuver him into a pin.

The only thing that saved me from one ripper was that I

had seen him go the night before against a callow college chap who confused collegiate wrestling with the real thing. Joe College wasn't even top caliber collegiate and the ripper didn't have to maim him to beat him easily. But he was a sadist and after getting the kid's arm isolated, put a double wristlock on it and then, after the kid quit and relaxed, the ripper took the lock past the point of no return, fracturing the arm.

Well, by the time I saw this bird, Omaha had done its work and I could pin, ride, and hook with the best of them (I never cared to rip, however). I'd worked with a couple of rippers and found that straight-arrow wrestling was something of an advantage in that you avoided extremes. It is harder to over-leverage than to put on just enough. So why bother? The simple way, in wrestling as in life, is usually the most efficient.

The upshot was that the next night I was first up. I soon found I had a helluva plateful. The guy had such a massive neck his head looked like part of his neck that had haired over. He had one ear beyond a cauliflower and was violence incarnate (shaking hands before the match he playfully mashed my fingers while winking at me). Worse, he also could wrestle.

Oh, he could wrestle. He must have had a date waiting for him because he hit me like a sandstorm engulfing a Bedouin. I thought I was in a gangfight for the first ten minutes. He battered me with his fists and elbows and leveraged me all over the dirty mat with his whiplike legs. His fingers were in my eyes so much I only got glimpses of him. If I'd seen more I would have been scared to death.

As it was I was only frightened silly. And this helped. It made me run like a thief and use every defensive ploy Omaha had taught me. If I had tried to stand my ground he would have pinned me in short order.

But it doesn't diminish me to say I ran. That night I could have beaten Bojangles Robinson going backward or "Bicycle Bob" Pastor going sideways. It was not strategy but simple unalloyed fear that propelled me around that mat like a wraith.

Either way, it paid off. Condition began to tell and after twenty minutes or so it was evident that the guy had included

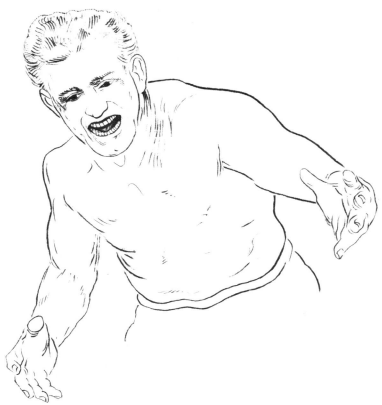

Jack Sherry, The Ultimate Shooter

too many broads and beer in his training regime. The cyclone became wind gusts and finally a faint breeze. Then I stopped running and started chasing.

Give him his due—he was about as good defensively as offensively. But I had survived Krakatoa and now I was hungry. I finally caught him, took a leg, and spilled him toward a pin. I had
him but, when he still wouldn't go, I stretched his neck a bit and
this did the trick.

Strangely, that stretching seemed to earn his respect more
than the pin did. We were now brother rippers. And as he shook
my hand he gave me the beautiful accolade: "You can wrestle

a little, kid."

With this background you can see how I came to love wrestling. I want now to digress on the institution a bit because it's never been done properly. There have been only three books of any worth written on it. Nat Fleischer's tome, *From Milo to Londos* (1936) was seriously marred by inaccuracies. A better book, though also flawed in places, is G. Kent, *A Pictorial History of Wrestling* (1968). By far the best is one published in Finnish in 1939, Heike Lehmusto's *Painin Historia (History of Wrestling)*. To show you how important the subject is to me, I actually learned Finnish sufficiently to translate this book for my research. *

I've pretty much stripped the narrative of all but essentials. The countries and wrestlers I've singled out for attention seem to me to be those most reflective of the flavor of wrestling at certain times. Obviously, I would have dealt with many more styles and wrestlers had space permitted.

The Ancients

As with boxing, I'm going to let the historians sort out the fine

---

*Besides these I used such specialized books as F. Doberl, *Ein Leben Auf der Ringer-Matte*, 1948; D. F. Draeger and R. W. Smith, *Asian Fighting Arts*, 1969; E. Gardiner, *Athletics of the Ancient World*, 1930; George Hackenschmidt, *The Way to Live in Health and Physical Fitness*, 1945; H. Harris, *Greek Athletes and Athletics*, 1967; W. Litt, *Wrestliana*, 1860; S. Mujumdar, *Strongmen Over the Years*, 1942; and C. Wilson, *The Magnificent Scufflers*, 1949. Some of the estimable research that R. W. Smith has done in preparing his seminal *World History of Wrestling* (still several years from publication) and the exceptional work of the late Mohammed Hanif of England have graciously been made available to me and have kept me on the track. And at a late hour another wrestling expert in England, Balbir Singh Kanwal, came forward to set me straight on data for which I thank him.

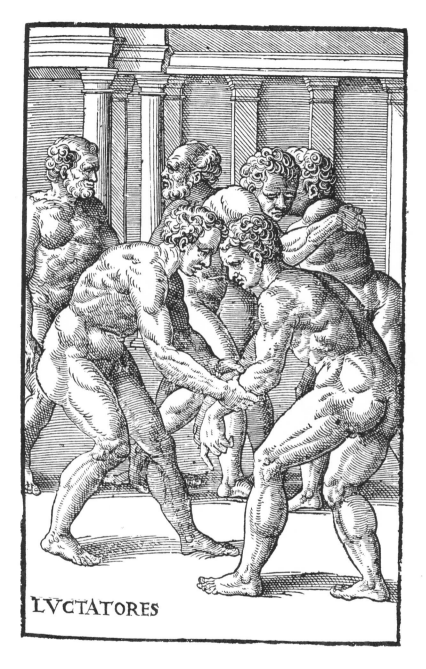

LVCTATORES

Wrestlers in Ancient Greece (Mercurialis)

points of ancient wrestling.* All I want to do here is to sketch a base for my more modern meanderings.

In ancient Assyria and Egypt, about five thousand years ago, wrestling was so developed that there are few postures known today that weren't already depicted on tombs (particularly at Beni Hasan, 2380–2167 B.C., on the Nile). These show a free-style standing, but not a brutish, wrestling. Later the form found its way to Greece where all classes of society revelled in it; even women wrestled. Most of the grappling was done naked, with bodies heavily oiled, and no weight categories.

I won't dwell on ancient Greek wrestling except to say that it was very much a part of the life of those times. Though the great physician, Galen, called it "depraved gymnastics," nearly everyone else was for it. Plato and Socrates wrestled and thought it salubrious for their minds. The law supported it even to the extent of declaring (Law of Ulpianus) that anyone who killed an opponent wrestling was immune from penalty. The Greek form was largely a standing type of wrestling; groundwork was a feature of the all-out pancration.**

Competitive wrestling started at the 18th Olympiad (704

---

* R. W. Smith has been working thirty years on a history of world wrestling. When it emerges I think he will find that among the national indigenous forms the Muslim was the truest international one. It travelled from Morocco to Mongolia, bareskinned and jacketed, was scientific in Turkey, and perfected in the Punjab. In Turkestan it was barbarous and often became a fight to the death. This form later evolved to Chinese wrestling (*shuai chao*) and judo.

**The aforementioned pancration which combined wrestling and boxing was introduced at the 33rd Olympiad in 648 B.C. Pindar and Thucydides saluted it for its comprehensiveness. Philip II of Macedonia, father of Alexander the Great, reportedly participated. One pancrateist, Arrhachion, was being strangled, but extricated himself for a moment and began twisting his opponent's toes. In great pain, the man signalled defeat and the laurels went to Arrhachion who had meantime expired from the effects of the choke. Polydamas of Thessaly was probably the

John F. Gilbey

B.C.). The best Olympic wrestler of the ancient period was Milon of Croton who purportedly carried an ox around the stadium, put it down, and killed it with a single punch. Six times victor in the Olympiad and six times victor in the Pythian Games, Milon was at his prime between 540–516 B.C. A pupil of the famous philosopher and mathematician Pythagoras, Milon was so strong he could hold a pomegranate in his hand and no one could take it by twisting his fingers nor was the fruit ever blemished. But in 512 B.C. against the younger Timasithesus, Milon was forced by exhaustion to give up. A tree rang down his final curtain—or so mythology records. Wedges had been driven into it for splitting. The mythological Milon attempted to tear it apart with his bare hands, the wedges slipped out, and he was imprisoned and helpless against the wolves that made a meal of him. The actual Milon's death was more mundane: he was done in by a band of thugs.

Wrestling spread from the Greeks to the Romans and the Etruscans. Perhaps the best grappler Rome ever produced was Melankomos, a favorite of Emperor Titus (A.D. 79–81). Later, the form spread to Europe and England.*

---

greatest pancrateist, but his strength fatefully defeated him. When the house in which he was a guest began to collapse Polydamas propped it up for a time but time told and when the house finally fell the strongman fell with it.

* This was merely one derivative of wrestling spawned in the Middle East. Remember the story of Jacob wrestling the angel? Apparently Jacob won the fight from which the very name Israel (thought to mean "a wrestler with God") came. The angel who wrestled Jacob wanted to call it quits at daybreak even though he appeared to be winning the match after pulling the Patriarch's leg out of joint (a devilish dodge). Jacob limped away but to this day orthodox Jews abstain from eating the part of an animal's body containing the thigh vein (the sciatic nerve).

Europe

What is variously called Graeco-Roman or classical wrestling should actually be called French wrestling. Chiefly a ground wrestling form placing priority on strength and endurance and prohibiting use of the feet and holds beneath the waist, it has little in common with the ancient wrestling of Greece and Rome. It came to flower in France in the nineteenth and the early twentieth century. But because it swept across Europe as the predominant form of international wrestling it is too confining to call it "French." Here I'll call it Graeco-Roman to distinguish it from free style.

All we know about Graeco-Roman wrestling until the nineteenth century is the probably aprocryphal account of King Henry VIII and Francis I of France going at it once hot and heavy. One story relates that Francis threw Henry; another, that the spearholders broke it up before a conclusion was reached. We know that wrestling was an adjunct of swordplay during this period, used whenever opponents closed. It thus became part of the knight's regime; even monks grappled in their leisure time. A. Durer, the famous artist, wrote one of the first illustrated books on wrestling postures in 1512.

Although documents are not too revealing, wrestling in France probably is as old as in England, and by the mid-nineteenth century it was in full flower. At that time the French had some splendid wrestlers. Bernard Mangelle (Father Bernard) was one. A cruel and vicious sort, he more than once got his comeuppance. When he was fifty-four he fought Etienne La Patre. He was ahead till the seventeenth minute when he tore a shoulder muscle after being thrown. The audience refused to let him accept defeat so Bernard didn't resist and was thrown many times, after which he crawled from the ring.

He had a challenge stall later at Bordeaux and once a sailor stepped up for a go. The sailor had shoes with nails protruding but wouldn't take them off. As a consequence, Bernard bled much, but finally threw the man and a general fight ensued. In 1877 when he was fifty-seven he fought and won his last match, this against the negro, Abdullah.

A year after Rambaud bested the British boxer Dickson,* a wrestler from Lyon named Broyasse went to America to accept the challenge of a giant negro. The negro got Broyasse (who died in 1872) in such a vice he was injured and gave up the match. In the rematch, Broyasse reportedly gave the negro an apple and said: "Eat this, it will be your last." After the negro ate the apple, they fought and Broyasse got a strangle on his head and killed him.

In France wrestling continued to develop, though bastard forms were often part and parcel of giant exhibitions featuring circus stunts, strength feats, and, sometimes, savate matches. With this venue, it was easy to resort to show wrestling.

A flashy Italian, Pietro Dalmasso (born 1852) though only 5'9" and 180 pounds was a popular favorite in Paris. At his prime he beat Tom Cannon, William Muldoon, M. Gambier, Sabes, and Carl Abs, all international champions. In 1897, however, Gambier, only 172 pounds, pinned Dalmasso, who hadn't lost in ten years, in three minutes. Two years later, Gambier wrestled a ten-hour draw with the tireless Michael Hitzler, another good little man.

But then the bigger boys began to come on. Paul Pons, France's best wrestler ever, ruled the roost in Paris from 1898 through 1910. After he beat the Britisher, Tom Cannon, in 1891, Pons was the toast of the continent. Standing 6'5" and weighing 285 pounds, he was beaten in Graeco-Roman only by Hackenschmidt** (three

---

*Rambaud was a savate cum wrestler. He kicked Bernard out in 1850 and defeated Arpin, who had only lost once in his life—to Marseilles the Elder—the year before.

**Besides Hackenschmidt, little Estonia also spawned Alex Aberg and George Lurich, truly outstanding wrestlers, making it perhaps the greatest wrestling country in Europe. Aberg had a hammerlock that wouldn't quit. He'd work out from atop, twist your wrist behind your back, haul you up from the floor, then toss you or turn you into a pin.

Paul Pons Top-Gripping R. Le Boucher

John F. Gilbey

times), Raicevitch, Hali Adali, and his own countryman, Raul "the Butcher." Raul, if he had not died early (1907), probably would have surpassed even Pons.

There were giants in those, the palmy days of Graeco-Roman wrestling, among the best being L. Pytlasinski, A. Aberg, L. Beaucairois, Petersen, G. Lurich, and D. Van den Berg. Let's look more closely at the top three: George Hackenschmidt, Stanislaus Zybyszco, and Ivan Podubny.

George Hackenschmidt

George Hackenschmidt was probably the greatest Graeco-Roman-style wrestler who ever lived. And one of the best free-style wrestlers as well. Born in Estonia, he early came to the attention of the Tsar's physician, Krajewski, more for his weightlifting prowess than for his wrestling. But in that period the two skills often went together, and before long Hack was notching victories over such greats as George Lurich and L. Pytlasinski. Turning professional, he beat Paul Pons of France in forty-five minutes.

Jack Carkeek, British champion in 1902, performed in music halls where he publicly challenged all comers, especially the "Russian Lion" Hackenschmidt. One night Hack showed up prepared to wrestle. Carkeek ran from the stage. Hack had come to England to learn free-style wrestling and to accept the challenge of the Turk, Muhammed Madrali. He forthwith went into training which consisted, among other things, of supporting six hundred pounds on his back. In the long-awaited match against Madrali, Hack pinned the giant Turk in a minute and a half: not bad for a Graeco-Roman wrestler learning a new system!

In the same year he defeated Tom Cannon, the Greek A. Pieri (twice), and the American Tom Jenkins. Three years later (1905) he beat Jenkins in Madison Square Garden to become world free-style champion.

Much controversy surrounds Hack's two matches with American champion Frank Gotch. In 1908 in Chicago, Gotch fouled him with everything but the water bucket and when the American

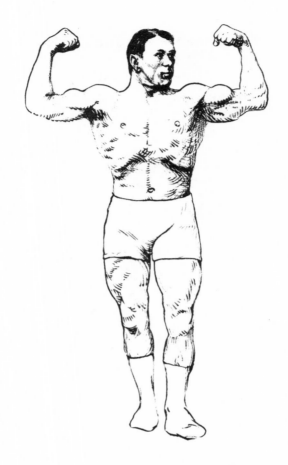

The Magnificent Hackenschmidt

referee to whom Hack protested would not right matters, Hack walked out. Jack Carkeek, Hack's old tormentor, had trained Gotch in the tactics that would upset Hack—and they worked. Gotch was oiled down like a Turk and Hack said he'd even soaked his hair in kerosene (since this would have endangered Gotch more than Hack it is difficult to credit the latter).

The *New York Times* of April 4, 1908, reported that "Gotch side-stepped, roughed his man's features with his knuckles, butted him under the chin, and generally worsted Hackenschmidt

John F. Gilbey

until the foreigner was at a loss how to proceed." Another account said that Hack "fearfully lacerated, his nostrils torn, his lips and face battered beyond recognition" quit because of "a dirty deal" (*New York Evening Journal*). Finally, the *New York Sun* reported that the victory "would have been more gratifying to our national vanity had the encounter been tolerably clean." So much for the first fight.

Three years later the two met again, this time before 35,000 fans at Comiskey Park in Chicago. Unfortunately, Hack badly hurt a leg in training and asked for a delay. Jack Curley, the promoter, fearful that he'd lose his gate, implored Hack to go through with the original date despite his leg. Hack did—although he announced before the fight that all bets were off—and, unable to maneuver, was pinned twice by Gotch.

When Hack was going good, he disposed of five wrestlers in seven minutes in Munich, five in six minutes in Paris, and six in eighteen minutes in New York. Standing 5′9½″ tall, Hack weighed 225 pounds at his peak. He never drank and seldom ate meat, believing that vegetables "put you in direct touch with the cosmos." In retirement he wrote six books, one of them with the formidable title *Man and Cosmic Antagonism to Mind and Spirit*, all of them hard going for me. He never watched professional wrestling, saying: "It is just rehearsed acrobatics . . . In my time, it was a clean sport, but now . . . well, it's not the sort of thing you would let your child go to see!"

When I saw him last the year before he died at ninety (1968), he still jogged a bit each day and was the picture of health. He spoke of Gotch without rancor and was thoroughly at peace with himself and others.

S. Zbyszco

One day a young Polish student visited a circus, took up the house wrestler's challenge, and threw the behemoth off the stage. This was Stan Zbyszco's introduction to wrestling. Blessed with a splendid physique (his biceps measured twenty-three inches!), he then met the great Pytlasinski* who took him to an international tournament in Berlin where Zbyszco won several matches but was injured by the Frenchman, LeBeaucairois. This drove him back to his studies, but he emerged again in 1905 at St. Petersburg where he wrestled a two-hour draw with the unbeatable Podubny. The next year in Paris he beat the Russian on a decision to win the Graeco-Roman championship of the world—one Zbyszco later claimed was never taken from him.

He continued to wrestle and converted to free style to take on Gama, Gotch, and others. In 1914, World War I caught him in Russia, but the regime treated him well and let him wrestle wherever he liked. During this period a top wrestler, Alex Aberg, accused Zbyszco of being an Austrian spy and challenged him to wrestle for $2,500. Zbyszco accepted. Aberg even had him arrested ("to prevent him from fleeing from my terrible holds") and escorted by guards to the ring. Zbyszco beat him badly, but there was so much tension at ringside as he was being escorted away he feared for his life. So he took the gold he had been presented for winning and tossed it into the crowd, escaping in the furor that followed.

In the 1920s Zbyszco came to America with his brother Wladek, won various titles (now blemished by show), and retired to a pig farm in Missouri where they both died in their seventies not too long ago. Wladek was also an exceptional wrestler. He took on Gotch in a handicap match in Buffalo in which the Iowan was supposed to pin him twice in two hours. At the end of an hour

---

*Inevitably the day came when student beat master. It reminds me of the story told by Saadi Muslih-Ud-Din of Persia (1184–1291) of a master who knew 360 tricks of wrestling and taught his best pupil 359 of them. When the student reached the zenith of his powers he challenged the master. Then it was that the master unveiled the 360th technique and threw the younger man into the ozone. When the victim complained, the master told him a truth, old even then: "Have you not heard it said 'No man learned the art of archery from me who did not in the end turn his bow on me?'"

John F. Gilbey

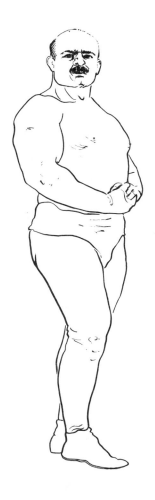

Stan Zbyszko

Gotch, unable to pin, lost the handicap match. Wladek, though he won most of his matches, never achieved the fame of his brother.

The brothers Zbyszco tried to save the sport from the fakes but had little success. I visited with them on their farm several times and invariably we'd get on this subject. They dated show from the time Strangler Lewis tanked for $115,000 to Gus Sonnenberg who knew nothing of wrestling. (Sonnenberg the "champ" later wrestled Dick Shikat, a darned good shooter. Dick told him in the ring: "If you want to keep the title, you'll have to wrestle for it. I'm not taking any falls." Sonnenberg later recounted: "I was in a helluva spot. After all, I had never wrestled before.")

Promoter Jack Curley got a handsome Greek boy named Jim Londos who, like Sonnenberg, couldn't wrestle even a little, and the combines were born. Good wrestlers had to perform or they didn't wrestle. After 1930 or so, shooting matches became even rarer than they were fifteen years before. At any rate in the 1950s the Zbyszco's challenged the whole lot of them and tried to get the U.S. government to quash the combines. These fine Polish wrestlers failed, and today the sickening joke is epidemic. *Fall Guys: The Barnums of Bounce* by Marcus Griffin delineated this scam back in 1937 and that exposé hasn't been improved on since, nor has its subject changed.

Man is a maverick in the animal kingdom and is puny alongside those we miscall beasts. But I still laugh when I recall "world champion" Bruno Samartino forgetting that he couldn't wrestle and agreeing to wrestle a carnival gorilla a few years back in Pennsylvania. It was the typical so-many-dollars for staying for five minutes. Samartino saw a woman challenger picked up and kissed on the forehead and deposited gently outside the ropes but still wanted to have a go at the behemoth. Beaten in a few seconds, Samartino remarked about it later, "It was the first time in my life I'd ever been kicked in the ass and socked in the jaw at the same time."

Ivan Podubny

The best of the Graeco-Roman wrestlers coming out of Russia was Ivan Podubny. In 1904 Podubny was considered a specialist in belt wrestling and accordingly was ranked low. Until then, Paul Pons of France was dominant in Europe, having beaten Tom Cannon and the 360-pound Turk, Norullah. At that time Podubny was working as a longshoreman. But then he started moving and won the European championship in 1906 and 1907 (Pons wasn't entered) and the world championship in 1908. He was past fifty

Ivan Podubny

when he was brought to America by Jack Curley. Like boxer Luis Firpo, he was as tight as tree bark and didn't trust banks. So he'd convert his cash into big bills and put them into a money belt which he wore into the ring. He had trouble converting to free-style but won some matches. His age and the new style, however, told on him and he was beaten by Stecher and Stan Zbyszco. He finally stayed retired after being beaten by Wladek Zbyszco.

England

Wrestling in England has a long history. As far back as the reign of Henry II (1152–89), contests were held annually on St. Bartholomew's and St. Jacob's Days. The eighteenth-century squire, Sir Thomas Parkyns (who died in 1741), would have no one but wrestlers as servants: this way he could try a fall whenever the spirit hit him. Parkyns was a queer fellow. Among other habits, he collected stone coffins as a reminder to his wrestlers that all were mortal and the great wrestler, Death, would have the final victory. (Stop to think of it, he doesn't sound so daft after all).

The Wrestling

England has several distinct styles of grappling, each one depending on the neighborhood. I've wrestled in all these styles against good exponents and can attest that each has its strong points and all are good fun.

In the Cumberland and Westmorland style the wrestlers take holds with the arms around the body, the right arm underneath and the left above, chest to chest. From this grip anything except kicking is fair game to bring the opponent to the ground. A man loses if his grip fails or if he is thrown, even to one knee. Dogfalls—where both fall simultaneously—are rewrestled. Most of its chips (tricks)—such as the back heel, outside stroke, hand, inside click—are seen in the other British styles, but buttocking is almost unique to it.

The Cumberland style may seem limited but if these codgers get a "holt" on you, write your will. Back in the 1950s I recall the South African terror, Jack Robinson, skilled in this style, who claimed to be able to beat anyone on earth (except his pa). Jack came to England, won the title up in the north, and came down to the Budokwai in London and ran their judo black belts off the mat.

John F. Gilbey

Wrestling in England (1832)

Lancashire wrestling, a free style, is the most popular of the three British methods because its rules permit everything except strangling and bonelocks. Among amateurs, however, the hammerlock, body scissors, and double-nelson is barred. A fall is counted when both shoulders touch the ground simultaneously or for a clean throw. The bridge is as key here as it is in Graeco-Roman to avoid a pin.

The Cornwall and Devon style, often called West Country wrestling, use jackets similar to those seen in judo. This garb assists throwing, but the scoring is made more difficult to compensate. Scores are reckoned on three points down: two shoulders and a hip or two hips and a shoulder. The determination of a fall led to continual bickering and lessened the popularity of this style. The old Devonian style used rough kicking, but that was abolished when the styles were merged. Groundwork was forbidden and, because of the fall requirement, a match would sometimes continue—with interruptions for rest—several days.

Wrestling in Cornwall and Devon had lost its popularity by 1900. At one time these wrestlers were regarded as the best in England. In the old days one started as a kid, there being a prize (usually a hare) for twelve-year olds. The players were scientific. However, the booted kicking that scarred so many legs led to bouts contested in stockings. The kicking was used "patriotically" by Devonians to counter the "Cornish hug."

In Ireland, perhaps because of the love of the stick and un-regulated violence,* wrestling was never popular. When played, the style was the collar-and-elbow of *Tom Brown's School Days*; a challenge was made by trailing a coat around the ring with the request that someone be good enough to "step on the tail of it." This style was exported to America but by the turn of the century had been displaced by Graeco-Roman and free-style.

In Scotland, wrestling was more popular than in Ireland. A combination of Cumberland and free style was popular here but turned out few wrestlers of international standard.

The Wrestlers

About 1550, during the reign of King Edward VI, a giant came out of the north country. A poor boy called Gilpin from Troutbeck, he bummed around the country with his mother, begging. Arriving in London, he tossed the champion off the stage almost into the lap of Edward. Gilpin had enormous strength and once it is

---

*To give you an idea of the pugnacity of the Irish, there is the story of the blind farmer taken for a walk on the old sod by a kind neighbor and abandoned abruptly when a bull charged. The bull, puzzled by a lack of fear, nudged the blind farmer who turned, caught the bull by the horns and threw it to the ground. The neighbor returned and said "Man I never knew you were so strong." "Right," the old man responds, "and if I coulda got that fella off the handlebars of the bike I'da thrashed him properly."

John F. Gilbey

said placed a thirty-foot long by thirteen inches by thirteen inches beam on the walls of a building unassisted when the workmen were off to lunch. But strength undid him in the end. He died at forty-two from injuries sustained in trying to uproot a tree.

Other great Cumberland and Westmorland wrestlers from the early period were Robert Dodd and John Woodall. Dodd suffered no rival before him for more than a few minutes. He could pick up a bushel of wheat weighing 150 pounds with his teeth and toss it over his shoulder. Woodall once lost the first fall and got so furious that he picked his antagonist up by the waistband and hung him to a strong hook on the ceiling! He drowned near Dublin in 1796.

Nearer our times, wrestling was characterized by its rural character and the fact that most everyone wrestled. There was little delinquency in Cumberland because the farm work in the daytime and wrestling at night left no energy or imagination for other things. Dick Chapman of Patterdale was only nineteen when he won at Carlisle in 1833 and George Steadman was well past fifty when he quit. Churchmen took grips with roustabouts. The jovial curate of Egremont, Abraham Brown, was so good with his buttock throw he is said to have invented it (he didn't).

Wrestling was a sport for all seasons. Melmerby and Langwathby were the Cumberland strongholds of wrestling where tournaments were regularly held since 1750. The Melmerby Rounds were held for two days on July 6 and 7 and the Langwathby Rounds for two days on January 1 and 2 each year. The major event in Cornwall and Devon was held at least from 1602 around St. Bartholomew's Day in August at Clerkenwell.

Buffs still talk of Jemmy Fawcett (1794–1804), a 145-pounder who would wrestle a grizzly. Against the 230-pound giant, Pakin Whitfield, Jemmy had to tie a handkerchief to his left wrist and hold the other end in his right hand in order to circle the mammoth back of his opponent. When Whitfield tried to draw him in, Jemmy "gait in amang his legs" and tossed the giant head over heels. Another giant toppled by Jemmy put it: "Jemmy Fawcett's neet a man at aw; he's a divil, a fair divil, and neabody'll convince me to thi contrary."

George Steadman Against Hex Clark

Will Richardson of Caldbeck was also a tough one. He won the head prize at the Fauld's Brow contest nineteen years in a row and between the ages of twenty-one and twenty-eight he didn't lose a single fall though he never missed a contest. There were other giants: Tom Longmire (the champion who showed Charles Dickens how to "tak' hod" in the 1850s); Adam Dodd, "the cock of the north;" John Weightman; Tom Nicholson; and Tom and Ralph Pooley.

And of course George Steadman and "Handsome George" Lowden. In 1877 Steadman won the heavyweight championship at Gramere and for many years it was either he or Lowden who

Donald Dinnie of Scotland

finished first. Steadman seldom lost and only once to a lightweight. Willie Park, all 133 pounds of him, upended big Geordie on an occasion never forgotten by British fans.

All of these men wrestled Cumberland style. The other systems pushed up their own native champions, but history has been stingy in recording them. One of the best Lancashire adepts was Tom Cannon who wrestled throughout the world with great success in the Graeco-Roman style.*

---

*Graeco-Roman was first exhibited in England by the Frenchmen Le-Boeuf and Dubois in 1870 but met with disfavor because of its lengthy and boring ground wrestling. Later, Paul Pons met the Turk, Memisch, at Canterbury and they reclined for three hours to a draw, putting the crowd to sleep. Graeco-Roman barred use of the feet, and to the British wrestler the feet were sweet.

Scotland turned out two great ones: James Scott and Donald Dinnie. Scott was the lightest man ever to win at Carlisle (in 1812), of "tight buildt, streight, [a] beany mak' 'iv a fellow without a particle o' lowse flesh about him:"

"Jamie Scott O' Cannobie
He hied to carel toon;
And many a borderer cam' to see,
The english lads thrawn doon."

Donald Dinnie (who died in 1906) will not die in the memory of Scotland. Near Kincardine O'Neil lie two massive boulders with rings, one 340 pounds, the other 435 pounds. I was at the Highland Games a decade ago when a heavyweight strongman picked up the "small" one in one hand. I tried and was just able to get it clear of the ground. But Dinnie could pick up both stones at the same time and walk five yards with them!

This dour outspoken Scotsman typified the cheese-paring propensities of his race. He would never perform except for money. Once at the Games, royalty came late after Dinnie had wrestled and the promoter tried to get him to toss the caber (a not-quite-regulation telephone pole) for them. Only if he got another two pounds, he said. He paid his taxes, he went on, and if they wanted to see him he'd have to be paid. He was.

Getting back to the stones, only one other man in history has duplicated Dinnie's feat. And that the strongest man since Milon of Croton—the French-Canadian, Louis Cyr. But Cyr outweighed Dinnie by over a hundred pounds. And Cyr couldn't run like a deer, toss the caber, and dance. Or wrestle.

Dinnie could. He learned the national style and the Cumberland but his prodigious strength plus his desire for pecuniary gain led him right into the international Graeco-Roman style where he was only a passable performer.

Last in the line is Bert Assirati, the best British shooter in the last forty years. Although he stood only 5'6", Bert packed 280 pounds onto his frame, being more a firehouse than a fireplug. He lost only once—to the Dane, Martinson, but later avenged that

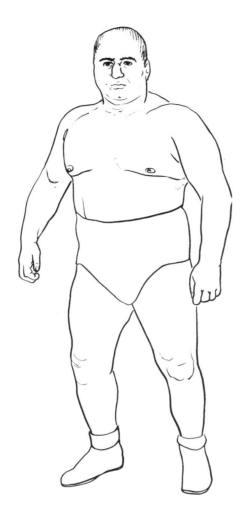

Bert Assirati

loss—in his first twenty years of campaigning. He drew in two tough matches with Frank Sexton, the best of the many American "champions." However, like other shooters, in order to get matches he was forced to show.

Thinking he was the world's best, Bert went off to India and Pakistan and challenged Bhollu. The great one laughed at him and gave him his nineteen year old brother, Akram, who promptly disposed of the Britisher. Undaunted, Bert tried conclusions with another of Bhollu's brothers, Aslam, in 1954 before 40,000 fans, but again lasted only a short time.

Later Bert worked for various nightclub chains in London. When a disturbance broke out at a given nightclub, he'd get a phone call, jump into his chauffeur-driven Daimler, and be whisked to the scene. Just the sight of him usually was sufficient to break up small riots.

Switzerland

" . . . Whoe'er would carve an independent way through life, must learn to ward or plant a blow."
      — J. von Schiller, *William Tell*

You all know or should know of William Tell, the man who, according to Carlyle, led "the first proclamation of Freedom in our modern world, the first unfurling of her standard on the rocky pinnacle of Europe." Von Schiller memorialized how Tell, the noted archer ("Tis early practice only makes the master"), ran athwart of the evil Austrian governor, Gessler, was forced to shoot an apple from his son's head, and said to Gessler: "Thou must away from earth—thy sand is run." And run it did.

Well, Tell wasn't a mutation; he came of Swiss ancestors "whose fists held lightning, and whose heart held God" (von Haller). And passed on the fighting spirit in the form of *schwingen* (swinging) the national form of wrestling dating from 1215. In a sawdust ring the strong of the village go at it in special short pants put on over their normal garb. The fighters engage by gripping each other by the trouser belts in the small of the back with their right hands and by the right trouser legs with their left hands. Each looks over the shoulder of the other and, from this position, they try to throw each other. When a man loses both grips or touches his shoulders to the ground, he is beaten.

Schwingen is done regularly at Swiss festivals, but the best

A Schwingen Maneuver

matches occur—and have since 1750—on Easter Monday. Two famous contests were held on the day in 1805 and 1808 in Unspunnen near Interlaken.

Mountaineers learned the sport exclusively from their fathers, but after the first book on the skills was printed in 1864, urban dwellers picked it up quickly. These stalwarts would fight anyone. One successful wrestler from Saanen said once that he'd even challenge the devil. Whereupon a stranger with hooves squared off with him. When the crowd stopped it, the devil said: "They stopped it just in time." To which the wrestler retorted: "Yes, I would have torn your hair out!"

Although it came to have scientific rules and applications, early *Schwingen* was so rough it was often banned because of the casualties (two wrestlers fell to their deaths over a cliff near Gampel and the hill to this day is called Schwingetotz "Death of Schwingers"). At the start of the nineteenth century, Neuhauser, a strong man of Wallis, challenged an old farmer from Auserberg who was disabled and had to get around on crutches. The farmer accepted on condition that he could sit during the swinging. Thereupon he embraced Neuhauser with such vigor that he had to acknowledge defeat.

And later a giant Britisher challenged anyone in Normandy for three hundred francs. Franz Wobmann, a swinger of Entlebuck, accepted. The Britisher tried to box, but the Swiss caught him around the body, tossed him cleanly, and donated the money to a noble cause in Switzerland.

Since 1895 there have been thirty *Schwingen* "kings." Early this century Hans Stucki was so named three times. The reigning king of *Schwingen* after World War I, Robert Roth, won the Olympic heavyweight title from America's Nat Pendleton in 1920. Four years later the pair fought to an hour draw in Paris. (Pendleton was an excellent wrestler and beat Podubny with a toehold in fifty-seven minutes in New York City in 1921.) Converted *Schwingen* wrestlers also defeated the American Olympic team 4–2 in 1928 at Geneva.

Iceland

I tried the national wrestling—*Glima*—of Iceland just once and was impressed. Historians trace it back into antiquity. Like Swiss *Schwingen* and so many other wrestling forms it was and still is a rural sport practiced at festivals and other gatherings.

Glima means "a flash," an apt name I learned in my lashup with a mere middleweight. Each of us grabbed the other's belt

John F. Gilbey

Some Glima Action

on the rear left side leaving the left hand free to grip the opponent's right thigh girdle. This put us looking over the other's shoulder. Squashed in like that, after a little moving around I grew restless and tried to stand up. Immediately the little blond guy came in with the Icelandic version of judo's *harai-goshi* (sweeping loin) and I left the ground. I was able to spin out so I lit on my side, but the point stood against me (any part of the body between the elbow and knee that touches the ground is a fall).

When a kindly old fellow on the sidelines told me this I nodded to my opponent and as we took grips again I resolved to get it back—and more. But he didn't give me a chance. There are twenty major techniques in Glima and this fireplug peppered me with all twenty in the next couple of minutes. Each was excellent in theory, but I sensed some were not too sincere, done only to keep me so occupied I couldn't attack. And occupied I was, doing what I abhor—using counters. But they were effective, particularly the sweep, and after a few he settled down and the practice petered out.

Glima hasn't converted well to the international style. When Icelandic wrestlers went to the Olympiad in London in 1908, they exhibited *Glima* (done well) and then participated in Graeco-Roman wrestling (done not so well). I can think of only one master —Johannes Josefsson—who was top-notch (he tossed the Japanese, Ottagawa, twice in 1913 in New York City). But why go to New York when you've got Reykjavik?

Russia

Russia is a big wrestling country with a long history filled with accounts of the sport. Many legends from the Kievan Period, a thousand years ago, contained wrestling oddments. Here is an exchange from the *Lavrenetsky Chronicle* (1022):

> Rededya said to Mstislav: Why should we
> sacrifice our bodyguards? Let us fight.
> Mstislav answered: All right. And then
> Rededya told him: But let's not fight with
> weapons—let's wrestle!

In succeeding documents we can glimpse the evolution of a systematic sport with competitions and good technique. Ivan the Terrible (1530–1584) watched a match from his porch:

John F. Gilbey

Patenechka stepped in quickly and grabbed Kostryuk with his right hand and pulled him across his right leg. Kostryuk was thrown high into the air and onto the ground.

This smacks either of *hizaguruma* (knee wheel) or *harai-goshi* (sweeping loin) of judo, depending on where Patenechka grabbed his opponent.

The Russian version of wrestling involves consideration for the opponent's safety. When Peter the Great (1672–1725) wrestled a young strong dragoon, the dragoon pushed him with his left hand and propped him up with his right hand so the monarch wouldn't fall. Of course there was some incentive here for safety, but many sources reflect similar consideration. The Berlin encyclopedia in 1794 gave this description of Russian wrestling:

> They try to throw their opponents chiefly by tripping. Some of the wrestlers had tremendous strength, but this method didn't require it nor were there many cases of broken bones or other serious injuries.

Technique was prized. The anthropologist, A. Tereschenko, wrote in 1847: "Skilled wrestlers win not through strength but dexterity. They first try to unbalance an opponent so that he can be thrown like a toy." Another anthropologist, Ravinsky, describes the "Moscow throw" in which the wrestler turns and uses his right loin against the inner surface of the opponent's left—clearly a Russian version of judo's *uchimata*. But it was not sufficient merely to throw: to win, the opponent had to be pinned (E. Pokrovsky, 1887).

Besides the Great Russian style to which most of the allusions above pertain, there were many forms of wrestling practiced by the various nationalities peopling that great land. These included: (1) Georgian "Chidaoba," a jacketed throwing form; (2) Azerbaijani "Gyulish," a free-style method culminating in a pin; (3) Tadzhikistani "Gushti"; (4) Uzbekh "Kurash"; (5) Tatar "Kuryash"; and (6) Armenian "Kokh."

The Tadzhiks still wrestle as they did in the thirteenth century with jackets held by a sash or belt and using the same varied trips and other techniques. The Kalmyks ("They fall to the ground as a defense against strikes"), Azerbaijans, and Georgians also used jackets. Pokrovksy wrote that among the Georgians, "It is a sin for a good wrestler to tear the clothing of his opponent," reflecting the fact that good technique was prized. The Buryat-Mongols and Azerbaijans seem to have favored legholds.

By the end of the nineteenth century, however, Tsarist Russia, concerned about the growing nationalism of these groups, tried to prohibit their wrestling. The ban didn't succeed: matches continued on a covert basis but without the cross-fertilization that matches between the various nationalities would have brought.

About the time Tsarist Russia got its first French development loans, Graeco-Roman wrestling was introduced at circuses. The "First Circle of Russian Athletic Enthusiasts" was established in St. Petersburg in 1885. In 1897, the first Russian amateur championships were held; these were conducted annually thereafter, with professional wrestlers also permitted to enter. Some of the masters of this classical wrestling were I. Podubny, I. Shyemyakin, N. Vakhturov, I. Laikin, and K. Bul.

In the Stockholm Olympics in 1912 a Russian, A. Klyein, was the best wrestler, though he had to forfeit his final match to the Swede, Johanson. The Swede had done little wrestling until the finals, but Klyein had wrestled four hours before his semi-final match against the Finnish world champion, Asikainyen. In that match the Russian had more *sisu** even than the Finn. Klyein went on the mat at 10 A.M., tired, with an injured arm. They fought seven and a half hours until Klyein threw the Finn to win. But the match had so depleted Klyein he could not come to scratch against the Swede finalist.

After the Revolution (1917) there was a more attentive audience for grappling. Exchanges occurred between exponents of

---

*Sisu is a Finnish attribute, an inner fire or superhuman force, surpassing fearlessness and extraordinary endurance. The great Finnish composer, Jean Sibelius, defined *sisu* as "a metaphysical shot in the arm which makes a man do the impossible."

A Samba Throw

the diverse systems. This not only helped the growth of free style and Graeco-Roman wrestling but also brought on a new jacketed form, *Sambo*. Officially established in 1938, *Sambo* borrowed techniques from Turkmen, Georgian, and other methods to become, finally, a giant synthesis. A hefty ingredient in this mix was jujutsu borrowed from Germany.

Although it had no official standing initially, *Sambo* grew out of a self-defense group at the Dynamo club in 1923. A. Spiridonov wrote the first text on it in 1933, but he failed to see its sportive value, stressing only its functional "street" use. At the same time, V. S. Oschepkov was popularizing judo and conducting bouts with wrestlers of various methods. He ended by abandoning his Japanese terminology and allowing his form to be absorbed into *Sambo*.

The first free-style tournament was conducted in the U.S.S.R. in 1945, and most of the prizes were won by wrestlers from Armenia, Georgia, and Adzerbaijan. These men were all trained in national styles of a fairly free nature and the Russian Graeco-Roman wrestlers could not cope with them.

Since then, Russian wrestling has surged forward on the world mat. Their grapplers are always in the forefront of Graeco-Roman, free-style, and judo wrestling. And given its heritage, Russia will no doubt continue to rank as a prime wrestling country.

Turkey

A wrestler who dies in the contest earns entry into Heaven just as surely as the soldier who falls in battle.
— The earliest Turkish commentators
on the *Koran*

Frank Gotch had two things going for him against Hackenschmidt in 1908: they were wrestling free-style, whereas Hack's style was Graeco-Roman, and oil. Gotch bathed in it before the fight. So Hack had to fight two alien styles, American and Turkish. Turkish national wrestling *is* an art of oil. The wrestlers wear leather parts, and every part of their body is heavily smeared with oil.

Over six hundred years ago, on his palace grounds at Edirne* (Adrianople), Sultan Murad the First began the Kirkpinar—the

---

*Murad was watching an archery contest. In commending a winner, he asked him how he had acquired his skill. The archer answered that it came from wrestling as a youth. Thereupon the Sultan decreed the annual festival.

John F. Gilbey

"world series" of Turkish oil wrestling. The sport is still waged in much the same way: barefooted, leather pants, and accompanied by frantic Turkish music. The winner is the one who drags his opponent three feet in any direction or throws him to the ground so that "his belly sees the sun." One fall decides things and it seldom comes before a quarter hour or so. The victor in the gruelling three-day event earns all the prestige he gets.

Even though soccer and basketball have recently stolen some of their glory, wrestling *pehlivans* (champions) are still recognized even in Westernized Istanbul.* Theirs is a long hard task. They have to have enormous strength because, even though they wrestle free-style, the grease makes for more pushing than pulling. Much effort is expended in holds on the heavy leather pants which, although tough to grip, are preferable to the greasy arms and torsos.

This ancient wrestling has produced some of the finest Olympic stars in recent years. And earlier in the century, it turned out tigers who would turn our current champions inside-out. After being beaten by Sabes, the Frenchman Doublier in 1894 went to Constantinople and hired three Turkish wrestlers: Kara Osman, Yousouf Ismaelo, and Norullah, and brought them back for Sabes to choose from. Unwisely, Sabes selected Yousouf. Sabes began the match with a furious charge which Yousouf absorbed easily. The Turk then turned Sabes head over heels onto his shoulders—all this in less than ten seconds. Paul Pons then took the three Turks on, beating Kara and Norullah, but losing to Yousouf (1895).

One of the few men Yousouf (6'2", 265 pounds) couldn't beat was his own countryman, Ibrahim Mammouth. Their bout in

---

* The other home of the mythical Sohrab and Rustam was Iran (then Persia) (you remember how, after beating Rustam, Sohrab unwisely lets him go and later is felled by the wily oldster). The Zor Khaneh (House of Strength) is an institution dating from before the reign of Darius. In the old days, when club and swordplay ended in draws, the fighters had to grapple for the prize.

Yousouf Ismaelo

Paris was the dirtiest seen since the Greek pancration. They locked, strangled, twisted, and ripped each other's noses for a while; then Yousouf started fighting dirty. In the sustained melee that followed there was still no winner and police had to beat them apart with sticks. From this Paris discovered the meaning of the old Turkish saying, "When men fight, women cry." The management took Yousouf to court where the judge asked Ibrahim if he wanted to sue. "Not at all," he said, "we have fought cleanly in the Turkish style."

Looking for new worlds to conquer, Yousouf went to America in 1897 and beat Evan "Strangler" Lewis. The next year he braced the American champion, Ernest Roeber. One account of this fight states that the Turk used a strangle which was barred and then went on a rampage, chasing Roeber outside the ropes. He finally caught him and threw him into the spectators for which he was

John F. Gilbey

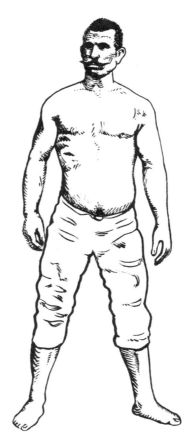

Ibrahim Mammouth

disqualified. Because Roeber, a Graeco-Roman wrestler, would not wrestle him free-style, Yousouf won $10,000 in gold.

The story goes that, putting the gold in a moneybelt and strapping it on, Yousouf went aboard the ship La Burgogne which was later wrecked. Some of the few who survived the shipwreck reported that Yousouf had acted like a wild animal, clearing a bloody passage through the frightened passengers. He jumped into a lifeboat being lowered, causing it to capsize. Although a good swimmer, Yousouf couldn't support the weight of the gold and went under.

The tough and skillful Kara Ahmed beat all opposition in

Norullah

Paris in 1899 but soon faded, losing to Hackenschmidt, Pons, and Pytlasinski. But Norullah, who, after being beaten by Pons, could not get any more matches in Europe, wasn't through.

In January 1901 he went to America for four months inviting all challengers to meet him there—Ernest Roeber and Tom Jenkins notably and Paul Pons especially. The 27-year-old stood 6'6", weighed three hundred pounds, and was a ripping cyclone. He might have let Bruno Samartino hold the ring rope up for him.

John F. Gilbey

In May he finally got Jenkins and Roeber to oppose him.

They weren't much opposition. He pinned Tom Jenkins twice in under ten minutes. The *New York Daily Tribune* reported: "Unlike other matches of this sort seen at the Garden, this contest seemed to be honest. Norullah with his immense girth and pointed head gave the appearance of a hogshead with a red-coated cantaloupe on top. No one could beat him." Two weeks later Roeber tried. Sort of. He hugged the mat and after twenty-five minutes when the Turk tried to turn him over by inserting his hand between his legs—a tactic prohibited by Graeco-Roman rules—all hell broke loose. Norullah was supposed to down the German three times in an hour but, frustrated by his stalling and the constraints of the rules, he began belaboring him at will and only desisted when twelve of New York's finest intervened.

Roeber himself was something of a ripper. On March 8, 1899, he got a hammerlock on the "Terrible Turk" (whoever he was), was awarded the pin but persisted in the lock until the "Turk's" *manager* gave up. That supposedly won Roeber the Graeco-Roman championship of the world. But against Norullah, a real Turk and a real wrestler, Roeber got out-ripped.

India and Pakistan

Oh, what wrestling there was in the old days! At the 1900 Exposition in Paris, the great Indian, Ghulam (5'9", 260 lbs.) came to accept the challenge of the "invincible" Turk, Cour-Derelli (6'5", 320 lbs.) for 5,000 francs. They met at the Hippodrome and Ghulam threw his opponent easily so that both shoulders touched. But the crowd wouldn't let it stop. And Cour-Derelli was intent on not restarting. He hugged the mat for 1½ hours. Ghulam insulted him and kicked him in the ribs but to no avail. Dr. Krajewski (Hackenschmidt's mentor) examined Ghulam after the match and stated that no one in the world could stand five minutes before him.

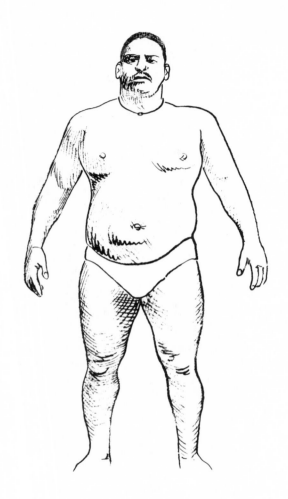

Ghulam

Success against Europeans was and continued to be a habit with the Indians. Tom Cannon was pinned in India in 1892 by the nineteen-year-old Karim Bux and by Ghulam's fearsome brother, Kaloo, in 1900. A decade later Gama took the American Ben Roller and S. Zybyszco into camp while Gama's twenty-four-year-old brother, Imam Bux, squared off with the formidable Maurice Deriaz in London. Bux was given little chance against Deriaz who had actually killed a man in the ring. But, unaware

124   *John F. Gilbey*

of the bets against him, Bux brutally pinned Deriaz twice in a few minutes.

What made Indian wrestlers so devastating? For one thing, they were big. Sometimes figures speak louder than words. Here are some data on the great wrestlers of the subcontinent:

Name	Height	Weight	Chest (normal)
Ghulam	5'8"	280	58
Gama	5'8"	250	56
Kikkar Singh	6'6"	460	80
Imam Bux	5'11"	230	—
Rahim Bux	7'	295	—
Kaloo	5'11"	260	56
Rahmani	6'9"	270	—
Goonga	6'1"	245	—
Bhollu	5'7"	350	56
Aslam	6'4"	330	54

They ate big and trained hard. A sample diet for these grapplers comprised: breakfast—six pounds of curd, two pounds of almonds; lunch—eight pounds of meat, soup with four chickens, and two loaves of bread; dinner—the same as lunch. Most abstained from spirits. At a victory celebration once, Maharaja Saya Ji Rao gave a grand feast for Gama. During the celebration he offered Gama some beer and got testy when Gama refused. So he offered him 100,000 rupees if he would drink one glass. Gama got up and departed, saying: "I will not sacrifice my principles at any cost."

They had technique, power, and fighting hearts.* You needed

---

*Wrestling wasn't restricted to the professionals. Rabindranath Tagore was typical of cultured men of his age in that he cultivated wrestling and music at the same time. Women also wrestled. Perhaps the best woman wrestler of all time was Hamida Banu who had over three hundred matches, only three of them with women. In thirteen years she was beaten few times and even offered marriage to any man who could pin her 235 pounds. The Buddhist canonical text *Cullavagga*, which forbade wrestling, didn't seem to have deterred many.

all three in India. Ghulam and Gama and others of their breed trained fifteen hours every day, doing 5,000 squats (*baithaks*) and 2,000 cat stretches (*dands*), working with up to fifty different opponents, wrestling for four hours at top speed, and then running ten miles.

The earliest epics, the *Ramayana* and *Mahabharata* (400 B.C.), speak of four great kinds of wrestling: the Hanumanti (from Hanuman of the Ramayan Epics, featuring adroit throws); Jamvanti (from the Bear king in the Mahabharata era who lost to Lord Krishna after twenty-one days of grappling, featuring locks on the joints); Jarasandhi (from the same area with stress again on locks); and Bhimseni (from the great Pandava warrior and brother of Arjuna—it features great strength and body slams).

For centuries these four schools dominated wrestling in Indo-Pakistan, until the seventeenth-century Moghul Emperor Aurangzeb sponsored an outsider, Ustad Nurruddin Pahalwan (the last word simply means "Champion"). Since Ustad became the father of modern Indo-Pakistani wrestling, three schools—Nurewala, Kotewala, and Kaloowala—have produced most of the finest competitors.

Nurewala

The pioneer school of modern Indian wrestling, Nurewala, goes back 350 years. Chiarag Ali Wala (who held Ghulam to a 2½ hour draw), Maraj, and Ghulam Mohiuddin were its prime representatives. The latter once went to Europe and pinned Maurice Gambier easily. No other Europeans would meet him and Gotch in America pretended not to hear his challenge. On the subcontinent he beat several of the best and held Rahim, Imam, and Gama to draws. Biddo, another member of this school, was the greatest Hindu wrestler since the giant Kikkar Singh. When Karim Bux, also from this stable, was only nineteen he flattened the Britisher, Tom Cannon, in Calcutta in 1892 and, after beating Kaloo, held the Indian crown for five years.

John F. Gilbey

Kotewala

This famous school produced such greats as Gama, Imam, Hamida, and the Bhollu brothers.

But before speaking of these, I want to pen a few lines on Ghulam, probably the best wrestler the subcontinent has seen and one who wrestled outside the established schools. Born to the famed wrestler Ali Bux of Amritsar, and brother of Kaloo and Rahmani, he fought four monstrous bouts with the Kashmir champion, the Sikh Kikkar Singh. Ghulam won the first and last, but drew the middle two. He was never defeated but died of plague at Calcutta when he was only forty.

Kaloo was the bad-tempered brother of Ghulam, second in rank to him. After Ghulam died in 1901, Kaloo took on Karim Bux Pelra, a fine wrestler who had easily disposed of Tom Cannon in 1892, but lost. After two more indecisive matches with Karim, Kaloo pinned him in three minutes in their fourth bout.

Kaloo met the feared Kikkar Singh seven times, and the pair were even until the last one. Then, behind in the match, Kikkar began to strike Kaloo, who promptly tossed him with a shoulder throw. The bout then became a pancration until broken up by the judges—Kaloo—who was better dirty than clean—giving as good as he got.* Later, against the court wrestler of Patiala, Chanda Singh, Kaloo was slashed by a piece of glass wielded by his opponent. Kaloo really mixed it then, and, blood streaming, threw Chanda heavily to win.

The greatest exponent of the Kotewala School was Gama.

---

*The rules for Indo-Pakistani wrestling are fairly flexible. The bouts take place on raked earth, with no penalty for going outside. A bout runs a specified time (say an hour) without rest, or until one wrestler has both shoulders immobilized. Locks are permitted; striking and kicking are not. But, as I said, the rules are flexible and dirty wrestlers were given great latitude.

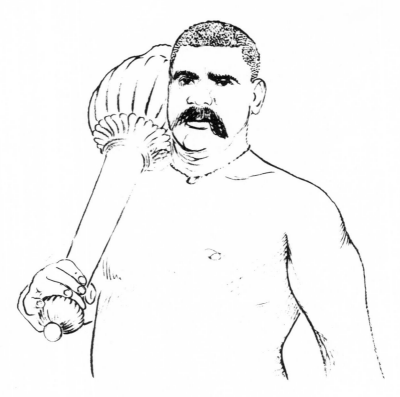

Gama

Born in 1882 to a wrestler father, Aziz, he began training at five.
When he was nine he went into a teen-age tournament of four
hundred competitors, and was among the sixteen survivors although so exhausted he was in bed for a week. At nineteen he
held the great Rahim and Ghulam Mohiuddin to draws. The next
year (1902) he pinned Ghulam in eight minutes and also pinned
the great Hindu, Biddo.

When Gama was twenty-nine he wrestled his old antagonist,
Rahim, to another draw. Then in 1910 he went to London where
he beat Ben Roller and Stan Zybyszco. He threw Zybysco three
times causing him to hug the mat until time ran out.

Returning to India in 1911, Gama met Rahim again. This
was an epic. The huge Rahim, his body powdered in red, was

Bhollu

out for blood. At first Rahim evaded Gama's favorite shoulder throw (*dhobi paat*) but soon the evasions were less skillful and he was running. Finally Gama scored with the throw but couldn't secure a pin. Coming to grips again, Gama hoisted Rahim up by a crotch hold, turned him, and was starting to pin when Rahim scissored his arm and was able to extricate. But then Rahim bolted the arena.* When Gama was forty-six the Pole, Zybyszco, challenged him. This bout occurred in 1928 in India and was over in a few seconds, Gama scoring with his shoulder throw.

Imam Bux was the brother of Gama and the man one had to go through to get to the champ. He was only beaten once in his career, shortly after World War I, by Goonga. After avenging this loss, he defeated the best, among them: Hasan Bux, Ghulam Mohuiddin, Rahim, and Kalia.

---

*Rahim, besides his matches with Gama, beat Karim Bux and Goonga, and at seventy-six in 1940 defeated an American wrestler, Hudson, in three minutes. Seven foot, 295 pounds, he fought five hundred times, lost maybe six decisions, but was never pinned. Following his second match with Gama, Rahim said: "After the bout Gama put his turban on his head with trembling hands but I was so tired I couldn't even do that."

Because of the famous Bhollu brothers the Kotewala School has been dominant since partition in 1947. Bhollu (Manzoor Hussain), born in Amritsar in 1922 to Imam Bux, was raised by his father, his uncle Gama, and the famed Hamida to be a champion. By 1949 when he was twenty-seven, he had fought two hundred times; since then he has never lost. He still reigned in the late 1960s but insisted that challengers beat his brothers—Aslam, Akram, and Azam first. No one ever got through that thicket.

Aslam, another son of Imam raised by his uncle Gama, may be an even better wrestler than Bhollu. He stood in the same relationship to him that Imam did to his father—he beat all the champion's challengers. He was undefeated as a youngster until in 1946 he was pinned by the great Yunus. Five years later, matured, he beat Yunus in seven minutes, then added Shareef and Kala to his string of victims.

Barnstorming south into India he pinned the huge Australian, Tiger Holden, in eight minutes and the Russian Ivan Timoshenko in four minutes—the same night. No one else would meet him until the great British shooter Bert Assirati accepted. In June 1954 the two squared off before 40,000. Assirati was upended in the first minute and slammed so hard he didn't gain consciousness for ten minutes. The Indian champion, Joginder Singh, and his number two, Tarlok Singh, fell as quickly to Aslam in 1961.

Two years later, the Canadian shooter, Paul Vachon, came to Pakistan and was paired with the oldest brother, Azam. Vachon, almost beaten, illegally used an elbow smash, temporarily blinding Azam, and then pinned him. Vachon was immediately challenged by Aslam. In their go Aslam cruelly manhandled Vachon, always stopping just short of a pin so as to lengthen the revenge. When Vachon couldn't get up, Aslam pinned him.

Near the end of the 1960s Aslam met the new Indian champion, "Tiger" Suchao Singh, and turned him every way but loose. And in 1967 Aslam journeyed to Britain and took on seven wrestlers, among them George Gordienko, who claimed to be world champion, demolishing them all in minutes. Asked about the opposition, this 6'3", 320-pound bear said charitably: "They are making a living my dear friend; life is hard."

John F. Gilbey

Akram ranks third to Bhollu and Aslam amongst the six brothers. He has beaten all the shooters sent against him. After the Lahore champ Bhola Ga'adi beat Azam, Akram took him on and demolished him. This loss by Azam was the first dint in the armor of the tribe and was reminiscent of the defeat the great deaf Goonga pinned on their father two decades before. It brought other challengers to the clan. Akram took them on. Haji Afzal, Sardar Khan the Afghan champ, Pyara Singh, Gurnam Singh, Vachon, and George Gordienko—a man the fake wrestling champions had side-stepped for years—all fell before Akram.

These men are direct descendants of the wrestling families of Kashmiri stock who settled in Lahore, Amritsar, and Gujranwala in West Punjab two hundred years ago. Since partition, this Moslem area (except for Amritsar) has gone to Pakistan; leading wrestlers who formerly were maintained by Maharajahs are now on state dole. In Lahore today there are over six hundred *akharas* (gyms) training ten thousand wrestlers. The Hindus in India play poor second fiddles* and it is probably true that the ten best freestyle wrestlers in the world now are Pakistani.

Kaloowala

From this school came such notables as Boota and Kikkar Singh. Boota from Lahore was never beaten and won the title "Rustam e Hind" from giants like Ramzi. Kikkar Singh got his name, it is said, by uprooting a matured acacia tree. Trained by Boota, he held the great Ghulam to draws twice and defeated his brother, Kaloo, four times. Goonga, made deaf by plague, also was a considerable man, being the only one to ever top Imam Bux (though he was defeated by him three times). Mhani Reniwala, a student of Boota and a real comer who pushed Kaloo and Rahim to the

---

*The Hindus were supreme until Sadika defeated Subdal and Ramdeb around 1840. Since then the Moslems have prevailed, only Kikkar Singh and Biddo among the Hindus attaining the highest rank.

limit, was cut off in his prime by a cerebral hemorrhage following his loss in a return bout to Rahim.

These Indo-Pakistani wrestlers then are worthy followers of
a tradition dating back to Sohrab and Rustam, the mythical wrestling champions of Iran and Turkey, and to the Prophet's nephew
whom wrestlers still invoke upon entering the ring with the words:
"Ya Ali!"

Japan

Sumo has entranced me since I read long ago in a dusty little library that Arthur Diosy, founder of the Japan Society of London,
was picked up perpendicularly and held over his head by a *sumotori* (wrestler) in Japan in 1899. (If you want to duplicate that,
put 130 pounds on a chair and reach down, grab two legs, and
pick it up.) And every time I'm in that fabled land, now undone
by technology, I watch sumo till my eyes hurt.

Ever since the first mythic match in 23 B.C.—the loser died—
sumo has been the grand big sport of the small Japanese. *Sumotori*
are surprisingly quick and have an endless variety of techniques.
The best are the grand champions (*yokozuna*) followed by the
lesser *ozeki, komusubi,* and *sekiwake* grades. Below these is the
senior division, from which Jesse Kuhaulua, an American from
Hawaii, moved up to *sekiwake* in recent years.

There have only been fifty-seven grand champions in history.
The first was Akashi (1600), a mere 8', 407-pound broth of a lad.
He and those who followed him trained as hard as any wrestlers
in the world—except the Indo-Pakistanis. They also eat prodi-
giously. Their single-course meal *chanko-nabe* is a giant stew pro-
viding about 6,000 calories per day per wrestler. Food is piled
in from the top and it takes a season or more to get to the bottom
of the pot.

Once a man becomes a grand champion he never loses the
rank. He is expected to continue winning, however, and if he loses

John F. Gilbey

Early Sumo

more than eight matches in a tournament he will voluntarily retire. In pre-war Japan there were two tournaments each year; now there are six: three in Tokyo, and one each in Nagoya, Osaka, and Fukuoka.

The *sumotori* sometimes trains eight hours a day. He learns to walk so that his weight centers on the base of his big toe. After a while his sandal wears away from the inside out, a hole is dug by the force. Even so, he carries himself as though he were walking on glass.

Sumotori are prized for their big hips (the leverage center), speed, and flexibility. All good ones can do a sidesplit, bend forward touching their chests on the ground, then stand—all this without using their hands. *Sumotori* have "groove strength," that is, an extraordinary range of movement in their joints. Added to pure "power strength," this lets them use an endless repertoire of "push" and "pull" techniques.

These huge men wrestle on a circular mound marked by a straw rope; the loser is the first to touch any part of his body except his feet to the ground or to be pushed out of the circle. This makes for rapid, vicious lockups and speedy conclusions. Slapping the opponent's face, kicking, and striking are fouls. Almost anything else goes.

Taiho (6'1", 352 pounds) became a grand champion at twenty-one—the youngest in the history of sumo. He favored the *tsuppari* attack, as mean-hearted a thrust as you'll ever see. Taiho is the only top drawer man to come along since World War II. In several contests he has done the unprecedented by beating all fifteen of his opponents without losing.

But, good as he was, even Taiho was not the caliber of Hitachiyama, who was peerless at the turn of the century. In 1908 at thirty-four he toured America and Germany and reportedly defeated everyone he met. This record has always puzzled me: where in either of these countries would he find anyone to confront him in his style? Nor could he have competed with Raiden who, despite his record from an earlier era, never made grand champion because he was *too rough* (!) or Ozutsu Man'emon (1870–1918) who wrestled nine years without a loss. Indeed, there were only seven grand champions for the first two hundred years because in those days you had to go undefeated for six years before making the grade. Clearly then, sumo like most other wrestling forms, is going downhill.

America

Old America was a wild frontier and the early settlers were not given to sportive niceties. Crude pugilism and wrestling matches were a fixture wherever a crowd could be gathered and bets taken.

Guns were always in evidence, decisions disputed, and sometimes the referee didn't get killed.

"I saw more than one man, who wanted an eye," a traveller wrote as he crossed into Kentucky, "and ascertained that I was now in the region of 'gouging.'" Another judged the inns he stopped at by whether the owner still had his ears—indicating that biting was also a favored technique.*

Thomas Ashe in his *Travels in America* (London: 1808) gives some of the flavor of early American fighting.

> Very few rounds had taken place before the Virginian contracted his whole form, drew up his arms to his face, with his hands closed in a concave, by the fingers being bent to the full extension of the flexors, and summoning up all his energy for one act of desperation, pitched himself into the bosom of his opponent . . . The shock received by the Kentuckian and the want of breath brought him instantly to the ground. The Virginian never lost his hold; fixing his claws in his hair and his thumbs in his eyes, he gave them an instantaneous start from their sockets. The sufferer roared aloud, but uttered no complaint. The Kentuckian not being able to disentangle his adversary from his face, adopted a new mode of warfare. He extended his arms around the Virginian, and hugged him into closer contact with his huge body. The latter, disliking this, made one further effort and fastening the underlip of his mutilator tore it over the chin. The Kentuckian at length gave out, on which the people carried off the victor, and he preferring a triumph to a doctor— suffered himself to be chaired round the grounds as the first rough and tumbler.

It is difficult to differentiate this milling between boxing or wrestling since it is clearly the American version of the pancration (which, however, didn't permit biting and gouging!).

---

*For an excellent survey on American rough-and-tumble fighting outside the ring, see Elliott J. Gorn's "'Gouge and Bite, Pull Hair and Scratch': the Social Significance of Fighting in the Southern Back Country," *The American Historical Review*, February, 1985.

But it was a grand country with a vitality only young gods are capable of. Listen to Mark Twain reflect it:

> Whoo-oop! I'm the old original iron-jawed, brass mounted, copper-bellied corpse maker from the wilds of Arkansas. Look at me! I'm the man they call Sudden Death and General Desolation! Sired by a hurricane, dam'd by an earthquake, half-brother to the cholera, nearly related to the smallpox on the mother's side. Look at me! I take nineteen alligators and a bar'l of whisky for breakfast when I'm in robust health, and a bushel of rattlesnakes and a dead body when I'm ailing. I split the everlasting rocks with my glance, and I squench the thunder when I speak! Stand back and give me room according to my strength! Blood's my natural drink, and the wails of the dying is music to my ear! Cast your eye on me, gentlemen, and lay low and hold your breath, for I'm 'bout to turn myself loose.

Early American wrestling was thus apt to be as wild as the vintage *Schwingen* of Switzerland or *Ringen* of Germany. But after the Civil War it began to take on a semblance of regulation and system. The collar and elbow style was imported from Ireland,* Cornish and Graeco-Roman from England, which, when added to the indigenous free-style, made for an interesting synthesis.

William Muldoon (born 1845), the father of American wrestling, was a broth of a man. From his early days when he got fifty cents a cord (eight feet long, four feet wide and high) for reducing trees to cordwood, he was as hard as the trees he cut down. In 1881 he wrestled Clarence Whistler for eight hours dur-

---

*H.M. Dufur, J. H. McLaughlin, and John McMahon were the champions in this form after the Civil War. The Cornish canvas-jacketed wrestling was popular with immigrating miners throughout the West. It was especially popular in Virginia City, Nevada, in 1860–80. And in 1900 among the transplanted Cornish miners in Butte, Tony Harris was acclaimed as "the best man to ever wear a jacket." But these specialized styles failed to produce any wrestlers of worth in Graeco-Roman or free-style.

Farmer Burns

ing which Whistler lost part of one ear extricating from a headlock. After beating Whistler and such other luminaries (as the Englishmen E. Bibby and Tom Cannon, the Scot Donald Dinnie, the German Karl Abs, and the Japanese, M. Sorakichi) Muldoon retired in favor of his protege Ernest Roeber. These two were the best Graeco-Roman wrestlers we produced: after them free-style came to the fore.

Martin "Farmer" Burns (he only worked as a farmer four

years) wrestled, barnstormed, and taught for forty years. Once he took a load of hogs to Chicago and while waiting to sell them took on two of the wrestling "pros" at a fair, pinned them, and picked up $100. He got the monicker "Farmer" because of the overalls he wore into the ring that time. The money was so easy he gave up hogs for wrestling. Born in 1861 in Cedar County, Iowa, he reportedly had five thousand matches and lost only seven. Evan "Strangler" Lewis beat him in 1886, but in 1895 Burns, outweighed by fifty pounds, turned the tables, winning the American free-style championship. Burns was the man who taught Frank Gotch and gave him his toe-hold speciality (Burns' best technique was the leg twist). He trained many other wrestlers as well.

On his fiftieth birthday, Burns pinned Oscar Wessam twice in Omaha and announced his retirement. At seventy-three, however, he tossed the intercollegiate champion in four minutes in an exhibition. In his later years he travelled with fairs, taking on all comers for $25 a head.

Two years after Farmer Burns won the championship he lost it (1897) to a one-eyed ex-mill hand, a splendid wrestler named Tom Jenkins. Jenkins deserves respect because he didn't dodge anyone and because he was a better straight wrestler than Gotch.

On the first point, Jenkins took on three terrible Turks and while he didn't win a match—losing two and drawing one—they never met a tougher man. Tom lost to the unbeaten Yousouf in an hour and a half and wrestled Hali-Adali to a three-hour draw in 1889. In 1901 he fought the giant Norullah but, while losing to the seven-footer, Tom beat him so badly that the Turk never again wrestled western free-style. Jenkins did all this at a body-weight seldom above two hundred pounds. His European trips helped convince the world that America was capable of top-flight wrestling.

But it was in America that Jenkins excelled. Here he continued to win, remaining champion until 1904. In February 1903 he easily beat the up-and-coming protege of Farmer Burns, Frank Gotch, the Iowa farmboy. Nearly a year later (January 1904), they fought again and this time Gotch fouled from the opening minute. He poked his fingers into Jenkins' eye socket (from which

John F. Gilbey

Tom Jenkins

Tom always removed the glass eye before a match) and also worked on the other eye. These tactics infuriated Jenkins so much that he clouted Gotch on the jaw and was disqualified. This lost Tom the title and he went around muttering "Gotch were't no gent," and plotting revenge. Failing to get his revenge in a match in early 1904, Jenkins braced Gotch in March 1905 in Madison Square Garden and regained the title. Two months later George Hackenschmidt defeated Jenkins in a straight match—fouls were fouls—at which Hack was unbeatable.

Two weeks later (May 1905) Jenkins again met Gotch, but

this time referee Tim Hurst called off all foul rules. The two Americans went at it no holds barred. Yousouf would have enjoyed it. After two hours of beating Gotch at his own devious game Jenkins won the deciding fall. Gotch was still out when they carried him from the ring a half-hour later.

Later, Jenkins lost to the younger man and retired to West Point where he taught until 1942 when he was seventy. Jenkins has always been made to take a back seat to Gotch. This is too bad. His record was as good as Gotch's. He was a better straight wrestler and beat Gotch at his own dirty hooking and ripping game. Moreover, he wrestled men the caliber of the great Turks whom Gotch never met. In a nutshell, both were our best freestylers but Gotch grabbed the glory because he was "no gent" in the ring. Jenkins has the lesser reputation because he was a gent. T'was ever thus I fear in this whirligig life of ours.

This is not to say that Gotch didn't deserve his reputation—he did—but only that he got it by wrestling a bit beyond the rules. He pinned his mentor, Farmer Burns, in 1899, and by 1901 Burns had taught the husky youngster all his tricks and Gotch was on his way. He won impressively against everyone (except for those losses to Jenkins). After a draw to Doctor Benjamin Roller in 1908 he took on Hackenschmidt and fouled the Britisher so that Hack forfeited the match. Gotch then went to Europe but fought no one of note there. Returning, in 1909, he defeated the Bulgarian, Y. Mahmout, in straight falls in seventeen minutes.* Later that year, Gotch reluctantly met the Pole, S. Zybyszco, and went to a non-title hour draw. In the return a year later Gotch got devious again. As the foreigner put out his hand to shake at the opening, Gotch dived under him, secured a half nelson, and pinned him. Gotch's behavior so rattled Zybyszco that Gotch was able to pin him a second time a half hour later.

---

*Mahmout was killed in 1913 by bandits in his homeland. He had come to America with a heady reputation and beat Charles Cutler, Gus Schonheim, and Fred Beall in jig time. His manager bet $1,000 that Gotch wouldn't be able to go behind him even once.

John F. Gilbey

Frank Gotch

Finally in 1911, Gotch again went at it with Hack. Unfortunately, Hack had injured a knee in training but was prevailed on to fight because of the huge gate. This agreement was sugared by his being told that Gotch had a severe neck injury and thus would be mince-meat for him. It was a lie and Gotch disposed of the credulous Hack fairly easily. Not too long after this Gotch retired, dying relatively young in 1917.

Could Gotch have beaten Hack in a clean fight? Never in the Graeco-Roman style: perhaps in the free-style. Give Gotch credit. Together with Jenkins he revolutionized wrestling in America. Where Muldoon and Roeber had been Graeco-Roman stylists, Gotch brought the free-wheeling free-style to the fore. He beat everyone he faced and had to turn to converted Graeco-Roman wrestlers like Zybyszco and Hack for competition. Could he have beaten Gama? Dirty or clean, never! But Gotch was top-drawer and after him wrestling in America went downhill.

After Gotch it became almost impossible to evaluate a wrestler's prowess because show wrestling overtook the competitive circuit. Say what you will of Gotch's tactics in the ring, he never entertained or tanked. He always wrestled on the level. Not so those who came after him.

We don't know for sure how good most of the Americans were because they seldom shot. Some, though, we can make educated guesses about.

Ed "Strangler" Lewis, despite Joe Stecher saying he couldn't have lasted a minute against Gotch, was probably pretty good. He started wrestling at fourteen in 1904. Mother Nature planned him: he had a twenty-one-inch neck and a swayback that set his thighs away from an opponent and gave him leverage. Thus he'd always be close to you but you couldn't get close to him. His best weapons were the hammerlock—which he used when in trouble— and the toehold. His much-touted strangle he used only for show. Lewis was supposed to be a great shooter. At age forty-five he shot against and beat easily Ray Steele (Pete Sauer, the former national AAU champ). Lewis wrestled five hours* with Joe Stecher at Omaha in 1916. When it got dark the ring was illuminated by car headlights and Lewis finally prevailed (it was officially a draw but Stecher reportedly acknowledged defeat). Even this match doesn't ring true. The papers said that Lewis put twenty-

---

*These marathons became commonplace and did much to hasten the coming of show wrestling. Gotch's caliber may be seen in the fact that he seldom took an hour to do his work.

John F. Gilbey

five headlocks on Stecher in eight minutes. If true, how did Stecher last? Lewis, like every successful wrestler of the period, submitted to show. (As early as 1922 John Pesek, a pretty fair shooter, was accused by his manager of being a member of the trust and his own record after that indicted him.) Lewis made four million dollars in the ring and died blind (from trachoma, the wrestler's curse) and poor at seventy-six in 1966.

There were other shooters, but most of them had to show sometimes to make money. Among them were Hans Steinke, Jack Sherry, Joe Stecher, Karl Pojello, Dick Shikat, Joe Montana (Joe had the best crooked head scissors I ever saw), Tony Morelli, George Tragas, and Fred Grubmier. In the lighter weights, to name just a few: Gus Kallio, Midget Fisher, Ad Santel, Tony Stecher, Clarence Ecklund, and Jack Reynolds.

Jack Sherry was a ripping shooter who had a wrestler for a dad. He came from Alaska to California thence to Omaha in the 1920s. He was pinned in an hour and a half by Lewis in 1932, but I doubt that it was a shoot. By 1939 Sherry was past forty with few losses—and I stress that those may have been "show"—and no one would wrestle him. We may never know how good this man was (a few years back I saw him working as a construction laborer in Portland, Oregon).

Fred "Legs" Grubmier was a good shooter. Because no one would wrestle him, Fred would hustle his skills for money. He'd size up a likely looking saloon in a strange town and drink soda pop out of a rye bottle all night, pretending to get drunk. Then this slight souse would challenge not only the bar but the whole blooming town. They'd usually feed him small potatoes at first and Fred would just barely beat them. Then, when he had the place roped and all the money bet against him, he'd pin the local champ twice in a minute. If, however, the ambience was really severe, Fred would contrive to make it closer. But he always won.

Karl Pojello started wrestling in 1912 and travelled for years in a circus troupe. Lydia Roberti, who flashed to stardom in Hollywood in the 1930s and just as quickly died, was also a member of the troupe. Pojello retired in 1939 but was induced into a "beat the Jap" match by a Chicago sportswriter in 1941. Going against the *judoka*, Mas Tamura, in a jacket match, Pojello, old and long past his prime, was choked unconscious.

Hans Steinke who died in 1971 at seventy-eight was a capable shooter. Known as "The German Oak," he came to America in 1923 and wrestled until 1940. He seldom lost a shoot but would lose occasionally at show. John Lardner, the sports columnist, saw Steinke wrestle Zbyszko and only once in a half hour was there movement—"when Steinke's nose twitched."

Which of the showboats could really wrestle? Frank Sexton and Lou Thesz were capable wrestlers but, because they seldom shot, it is difficult to assess them as shooters. It is easier to judge others. Many of the acrobats and handsome pro champions knew next to nothing about wrestling science. Remember how invincible the Greek Andonis, Jim Londos, was? Well, he wasn't. He shot only once in his life. And, as the French say, poorly. John Pesek (damned, he had a fine double wristlock!) using an assumed name got Londos inside the ropes once—in Omaha, if I remember correctly. Londos didn't recognize the face but sure did recognize the moves and quit the ring as soon as he could exhale.

In the 1930s an obscure Finn named Otto Huhtanen toured America and beat everyone who would face him. Not many would. He was a good shooter, not a great one, but still good enough to take anyone we had. And please don't ask me about our current crop. I haven't seen a decent American wrestler in four decades. Now that illusion is king in America—Rambo and Reagan ride high—fake wrestling is more popular than ever. And it's a crying shame!

Mixing Methods

It is difficult to compare men who wrestled in different systems. Some Graeco-Roman grapplers were able to convert to free-style, but there were fewer able to go the other way. True, the Turks came from their national ground system to Europe, stood up, and did well, as much from ferocity as technique. And the Indians could go from their dirt pits to mats and, because theirs was a free-style, dominate westerners.

But you can't compare sumo champions with Graeco-Roman or, especially, free-style adepts because of the disparity of rules. Because sumo is a short full-energy standing form, a Graeco-Roman style wrestler could have mitigated its effort by hugging the mat. Down there the *sumotori* would have been almost powerless. And a free-style wrestler like Gotch, if he could have escaped the initial sumo onslaught and got him off his feet (a big "if" for Graeco-Roman as well as free-style wrestlers), operating against the legs, he would have turned the Japanese fairly easily. Once turned on his back the *sumotori* would have been like a turtle. Reverse the scenario though and try to picture Hack or Gotch or Gama or Yousouf clashing with Hitachiyama or Taiho under sumo rules. They would go quickly.

There is an old story about a sumo versus jujutsu go in which the big sumo man picks the *jujutsuka* up over his head and says "Gotcha!" The *jujutsuka* responds "Yeah, but wait till you try to put me down and I'll kick you to death!" Which sent the *sumotori* out screaming into the night, the *jujutsuka* still in his arms.

Good wrestlers trying to wrestle in alien styles have had a tough time. Pytlasinski started as a belt wrestler and was unbeatable in that style. Put a judo jacket on him and he probably would have functioned well. Hackenschmidt and Zbyszco told me that they had wrestled jacketed and emerged unscathed and those two you had to believe. But these are exceptions. The Russians have done well in international judo because of their wrestling ability but they still fall short of the Japanese. Moreover, the American free-style tradition has not helped our judo.

An interesting discussion on the merits of jujutsu versus wrestling was held between H. F. Leonard, an excellent wrestler and protege of William Muldoon, and K. Higashi in 1905.* It was

---

*George Bothner, an excellent American lightweight, wrestled Higashi with jackets and reportedly won in three falls after be-

printed in *The Cosmopolitan* in May of that year. After seeing various techniques of jujutsu, Leonard concludes: "But I have yet to see anything that you can show me which we would not match here in America, and in some respects improve upon." Higashi responds: "But I cannot show you our serious tricks." Leonard, skeptically: "Ah!"

Leonard, instructor of wrestling at the New York Athletic Club for twenty years and author of a textbook on the subject, summarized his opinion of jujutsu this way:

> I say with emphasis and without qualification that I have been unable to find anything in jujitsu which is not known to Western wrestling. So far as I can see, jujitso is nothing more than an Oriental form of wrestling. It is a boast of the exploiters of ju-jitsu that through it any weakling could render helpless even a well-trained athlete, and that, too, without inflicting any injury whatever upon the victim. It would be an entertaining day in my life indeed were I to see such a feat accomplished.

He was killed by lightning in 1914.
Higashi said this of American wrestling:

> American wrestlers are strong—much stronger than any of us pretend to be in muscular strength. After all, however, wrestling is wrestling. Against jujitsu it is mere child's-play. I have

---

ing tossed twice in a row with *tomoenage* (stomach throw) at the outset. But the descriptions of the fight don't ring true. If it was straight-arrow, it merely shows that Higashi was not all that good in judo. A good judo man will usually throw a wrestler if the latter puts on a jacket. Unless, of course the wrestler cross-trains in judo. We know for a fact that Bothner showed on occasion. On December 15, 1914, he was one pin down and being eaten alive by the Japanese, Miyake. Suddenly he got good and pinned his opponent. Bothner was then forty-eight, smoking three cigars a day. It was so obviously hippodrome that it casts doubt on his earlier match with Higashi.

John F. Gilbey

met a number of Western wrestlers, and they are as helpless as babes against the art of jujitsu. And no one versed in the art of jujitsu is mad enough to expect anything else.

Boxer Versus Wrestler

I touched on the old question of boxer-versus-wrestler briefly earlier, but let me here cite some more chapter and verse for my belief that you should always bet the wrestler.

Sure, there are cases of mixed matches in which the boxer seems to have prevailed. Offhand I can think of only three. I've heard that Packey O'Gatty, a darned good bantam boxer when he retired in 1928 beat the *jujutsuka*, Shimakado, in Yokohama the next year (suspect because I've never been able to verify that O'Gatty was ever in Japan). In the second case, Bill Paul tells me that great black boxer Sam McVey beat a *jujutsuka* named Masuda in Paris in 1910.

Perhaps. It could happen especially with potent punchers like O'Gatty and McVey. I know for a fact that one very good boxer beat one very good wrestler. In 1901 in Dawson City, Alaska, a young Frank Gotch threw Frank Slavin, the Australian heavyweight, a couple times but was then knocked out. So it can happen (mitigating this, keep in mind that Slavin was also a good wrestler).

But don't bet on it. I've already written of how important wrestling was in pugilism. Paddy Ryan was so good at it he was able to win the world's championship in only his second boxing bout. And, despite John L. Sullivan's prowess in wrestling, the only man who ever terrified him was William Muldoon, the American wrestling champ who trained Sullivan for his fight with Jake Kilrain.

Jack Dempsey matched up early in his career with a wrestler and got thrashed. So, when Strangler Lewis challenged Jack in 1922 (*New York Times*, March 17), Jack didn't read the paper and didn't heed the challenge.

John Pesek, a pretty complete shooter of the 1930s, would take any boxer who would present himself. Big George Godfrey, the giant negro contender, tried him in 1936 and Pesek pinned him twice in eight minutes. A bit later, Joe Louis' front men came out pushing for publicity by challenging wrestlers to mixed bouts. They weren't serious, but Pesek answered the noise by betting $50,000 that he would pin Joe within five minutes. Joe's folks didn't accept.

Ray Steele, a journeyman wrestler of no great ability, tore Kingfish Levinsky, a heavy who'd beaten Sharkey, Loughran, and Slattery, in two in St. Louis in 1935, squashing him easily in thirty-five seconds. Kingfish wasn't too bright and went right out and challenged Bill Demetral, another shooter, who put the clamp on him in short order.

Even small wrestlers like Martin Ludecke, Gus Clem, and Jack Reynolds took on boxers fifty pounds heavier and never lost. Reynolds said that they were such poor opposition that you couldn't get fans to come to mixed matches.

Making it a bit more current, M. Kimura, the greatest judoka of this century, came to Hawaii in 1950 offering $1,000 to anyone in any system who could beat him. Other than two Hawaiians who bit the dust in less than thirty seconds, he could get no takers and returned to Japan in disgust. Shortly after, he teamed with Rikidozan, a former *sumotori* sekiwake, in pro wrestling back in his homeland. Later, Rikidozan lost his life to a knife in the men's room of his nightclub in Tokyo.

But when they put an overrated boxer like Ali in the ring in 1976 with so-called wrestler Inoki, a Brazilian field hand whose forte was throwing the discus, you get farce. Promoters paired this mediocre boxer and sham rassler in Tokyo and even as banditry it was bad. Ali knew that a wrestler will invariably beat a boxer in a mixed match—but he didn't know that Inoki couldn't wrestle. So Ali hugged the ropes and threw only five jabs in fifteen rounds. Inoki stayed defensively on his back throughout. Thus, the putative battle was never joined. Predictably, this smeller elicited boos and cushions from the audience. One boxing buff

was heard to comment: "Bring back the good old fashioned dive!"
And a Japanese wag remarked that if that latter-day samurai Yukio
Mishima were alive, he'd commit suicide again.